Discussing Cannabis

Editor: Danielle Lobban

Volume 399

First published by Independence Educational Publishers

The Studio, High Green

Great Shelford

Cambridge CB22 5EG

England

© Independence 2022

Copyright

This book is sold subject to the condition that it shall not, by way of trade or otherwise, be lent, resold, hired out or otherwise circulated in any form of binding or cover other than that in which it is published without the publisher's prior consent.

Photocopy licence

The material in this book is protected by copyright. However, the purchaser is free to make multiple copies of particular articles for instructional purposes for immediate use within the purchasing institution. Making copies of the entire book is not permitted.

ISBN-13: 978 1 86168 858 3

Printed in Great Britain

Zenith Print Group

Contents

Chapter 1: About Cannabis
Cannabis	1
Cannabis: the facts	4
Legalising cannabis will create jobs – and save lives	6
Differences between cannabis laws in the US and the UK	8
10% of teenagers have tried hard drugs by age 17	9
Illegal drug use by young people is more than double official estimates, major study reveals	11
Cannabis misuse	12
Cannabis strength soars over past half century – new study	13

Chapter 2: Cannabis Use
The effects of marijuana on your brain and body	14
Smoking cannabis just once can change a teenager's brain	16
Are weed hangovers real? Expert reveals all	17
How does smoking marijuana affect academic performance?	18
Mental health and cannabis	20
Cannabis users at 'much higher' risk of developing poor mental health	22
Cannabis users five times more likely to have suicidal thoughts, study finds	23
How does cannabis use affect sleep duration?	24
Cannabis triggered my derealisation disorder	25
Cannabis-impaired driving: here's what we know about the risks of weed behind the wheel	26
Cannabis: increased schizophrenia risk in young people linked to both low and high use	28
$13 billion US cannabis production industry 'damaging environment', study finds	29

Chapter 3: Cannabis as Medicine?
Is medical cannabis really a magic bullet?	30
Medicinal cannabis: what is it and is it legal in the UK?	33
Legal cannabis: why only 18 people have been given a prescription in the UK despite the law changing	34
Medicinal cannabis campaigners 'closely linked' with recreational supporters	35
How many people have tried cannabis-extract products?	36
Cannabis has great medical potential. But don't fall for the CBD scam	38
Where can I find help?	39

Key Facts	40
Glossary	41
Activities	42
Index	43
Acknowledgements	44

Introduction

Discussing Cannabis is Volume 399 in the **issues** series. The aim of the series is to offer current, diverse information about important issues in our world, from a UK perspective.

DISCUSSING CANNABIS

With almost a third of young people having tried cannabis, this book looks at the risks involved in using the drug, such as the effects on the mind and body. It also looks at the laws in the UK surrounding cannabis use, and when cannabis products can be used legally.

OUR SOURCES

Titles in the **issues** series are designed to function as educational resource books, providing a balanced overview of a specific subject.

The information in our books is comprised of facts, articles and opinions from many different sources, including:

- Newspaper reports and opinion pieces
- Website factsheets
- Magazine and journal articles
- Statistics and surveys
- Government reports
- Literature from special interest groups.

A NOTE ON CRITICAL EVALUATION

Because the information reprinted here is from a number of different sources, readers should bear in mind the origin of the text and whether the source is likely to have a particular bias when presenting information (or when conducting their research). It is hoped that, as you read about the many aspects of the issues explored in this book, you will critically evaluate the information presented.

It is important that you decide whether you are being presented with facts or opinions. Does the writer give a biased or unbiased report? If an opinion is being expressed, do you agree with the writer? Is there potential bias to the 'facts' or statistics behind an article?

ASSIGNMENTS

In the back of this book, you will find a selection of assignments designed to help you engage with the articles you have been reading and to explore your own opinions. Some tasks will take longer than others and there is a mixture of design, writing and research-based activities that you can complete alone or in a group.

FURTHER RESEARCH

At the end of each article we have listed its source and a website that you can visit if you would like to conduct your own research. Please remember to critically evaluate any sources that you consult and consider whether the information you are viewing is accurate and unbiased.

Useful Websites

www.bath.ac.uk	www.talktofrank.com
www.birmingham.ac.uk	www.telegraph.co.uk
www.castlecraig.co.uk	www.theconversation.com
www.independent.co.uk	www.theguardian.com
www.inews.co.uk	www.themix.org.uk
www.netdoctor.co.uk	www.thestudentlawyer.com
www.nhs.uk	www.ucl.ac.uk
www.ons.gov.uk	www.yougov.co.uk
www.openaccessgovernment.org	

Chapter 1
About Cannabis

Cannabis

Cannabis is a plant-based drug. It can be smoked, eaten or vaped.

How the drug works varies from person to person.

How it looks, tastes and smells

What does it look like?

Soft black resin, furry green leaves and hard brown lumps, cannabis can look very different depending on its type – but it all comes from cannabis plants.

You're most likely to come across these types:

Weed

Also known as grass, weed is made from drying out the leaves and flowering parts of the cannabis plant. It can look like dried herbs and is usually brownish-green in colour.

Skunk

This is the name given for particular strains of grass that are very strong. Skunk's become very popular in recent years and is often bright, pale or dark green in colour and covered in tiny crystals.

Hash/hashish

Not nearly as common as it used to be, hash (or hashish) is made from the resin of the cannabis plant and can be black, brown, soft or hard – depending on the type.

Cannabis oil

This is a dark, sticky and honey-coloured substance that's much less common than other types.

'Dab'/'shatter'

These are highly concentrated forms of cannabis that are extracted using butane. They come in a solid form known as 'dab' or 'shatter' and can be used as e-liquids in vape pens.

What does it taste/smell like?

Cannabis has a musky, sweet smell. Some of the more potent types of cannabis can have a stronger smell, but this isn't a reliable guide to the strength of any particular batch.

How do people take it?

Smoke spliffs

In the UK, most people mix it with tobacco and roll it into a cannabis cigarette known as a spliff or joint. Some people don't use tobacco at all and make weed-only spliffs - either because they prefer it that way or to avoid becoming dependent on nicotine.

Smoke bongs

Users do this mix by mixing the drug with tobacco and putting it in a pipe, lighting it, and then inhaling the smoke through water out of a large tube. There are many types of bongs, and not everyone uses tobacco. Like with joints, using tobacco in bongs increases the risk of nicotine dependence.

Eat and drink it (edibles)

People do this by mixing it into cakes (hash brownies), tea, yoghurt or sweets (gummies/lollipops). The amount

Cannabis

Cannabis is a plant-based drug. It can be smoked, eaten or vaped.

Also called:

Bhang	Hashish	Resin
Bud	Herb	Sensi
Dope	Marijuana	Sinsemilla
Draw	Pollen	Skunk
Ganja	Pot	Weed
Grass	Puff	
Hash		

Source: FRANK

of cannabis in these products can vary greatly and sometimes other harmful drugs are added too. The effects of consuming edibles are unpredictable and it can be very easy to accidentally take a larger dose than you wanted to.

Vape it

This method has become more popular in recent years. Most people use a vaporiser which heats the cannabis, rather than burning it. Very little is known about the health impact of vaping cannabis.

Smoking cannabis with tobacco increases the risk of becoming dependent on nicotine. To avoid this, don't use tobacco in bongs and spliffs.

How it feels

How does it make you feel?

The effects of cannabis can vary massively. Some people say feeling 'stoned' makes them feel chilled out and happy in their own thoughts, while others say it makes them giggly and chatty. But it can also make people feel lethargic, unmotivated and some people become paranoid, confused and anxious.

The sort of experience you have depends on a lot of things like:

- the kind of person you are (e.g. outgoing or shy)
- the mood you're in (if you're feeling down it will probably make you feel worse)
- the environment you're in (you're more likely to feel paranoid or anxious if you don't feel comfortable where you are or if you're with people you don't trust)
- how much THC it has (the main psychoactive compound in cannabis)
- how much CBD it has (which is thought to make users less likely to feel anxious and paranoid)
- how much you take
- how often you take it

Cannabis changes how you think and some people say it gives them a different perspective on things. It does affect your judgement though and people often think conversations or thoughts they have (whether good or bad) are much more deep or important when they're stoned than they would do normally.

It can also make you hungry, known as having 'the munchies', or make you feel sick, known as 'a whitey'. It can make you feel drowsy or sleepy and can give you the sense that time is slowing down.

THC & CBD

The hallucinogenic effects of cannabis are mainly due to a compound in cannabis called THC (tetrahydrocannabinol).

The other important compound in cannabis is CBD (cannabidiol). Skunk and other forms of strong cannabis contain high levels of THC but very little, or no, CBD.

It's thought that CBD can balance out some of the effects of THC and make users less likely to feel anxious and paranoid. You can't tell from looking or smelling cannabis whether there's a balance of CBD and THC in it, but in general, hash may have more CBD than skunk.

How does it make people behave?

Cannabis can make some people giggly and chatty, and other people paranoid, confused and anxious – it really depends on the type of person taking it and the circumstances they take it under.

Some people:

- Experience mild hallucinations if they take particularly strong cannabis.
- Become lethargic and unmotivated.
- Have problems concentrating and learning new information. This is because studies suggest that cannabis affects the part of the brain we use for learning and remembering things.
- Perform badly in exams. Because cannabis impacts the part of the brain we use for learning and remembering things, regular use by young people (whose brains are still developing) has been linked to poor exam results.

Duration

How long the effects last and the drug stays in your system depends on how much you've taken, your size and what other drugs you may have also taken.

To kick in:

When smoked, it normally takes a minute or two to feel stoned. If you eat cannabis, it can up to an hour.

How long it lasts:

This depends on how much you smoke. Generally, the effect is strongest for about 10 minutes to half an hour after smoking cannabis, but if you smoke a lot, you may still feel stoned for a couple of hours. If you eat cannabis, the peak effects can last for 2 to 4 hours, and there may even be a few more hours before the effects wear off completely.

After effects:

People may still feel the effects the next day, particularly after a heavy session.

How long will it be detectable?

If you've used cannabis as a one-off, it will show up in a urine test for around 2 to 3 days afterwards.

However, this can go up to a month for regular users.

How long a drug can be detected for depends on how much is taken and which testing kit is used. This is only a general guide.

The risks

Physical health risks

Smoking cannabis can:

- make you wheeze and out of breath
- make you cough uncomfortably or painfully
- make your asthma worse if you have it

There's been less research on it but smoking cannabis is likely to have many of the long term physical health risks as smoking tobacco (even if you don't mix the cannabis with tobacco). So smoking cannabis can also:

- increase the risk of lung cancer
- increase your heart rate and affect your blood pressure, which makes it particularly harmful for people with heart disease

- reduce your sperm count if you're male, affecting your ability to have children
- suppress your ovulation if you're female, affecting your ability to have children
- increase the risk of your baby being born smaller than expected if you smoke it while pregnant

Mental health risks

Using cannabis can:

- affect your motivation to do things
- impair your memory so you can't remember things or learn new information
- give you mood swings
- disturb your sleep and make you depressed
- make you anxious, panicky, or even aggressive
- make you see or hear things that aren't there (known as hallucinating or tripping)
- cause hours (or days) of anxiety, paranoia and hallucinations, which only settle down if the person stops taking it – and sometimes don't settle down at all
- cause a serious relapse for people with psychotic illnesses like schizophrenia
- increase your chances of developing illnesses like schizophrenia, especially if you have a family background of mental illness and you start smoking in your teenage years

What is cannabis cut with?

Lots of things. Dealers cut hash with similar-looking substances or heavy materials to increase the weight of the drug and make a bigger profit.

Although not all cannabis is cut, it's very hard to know when it is or isn't – so you could be smoking, eating or vaping chemicals from all sorts of unknown substances, including pesticides used when growing the cannabis.

Tobacco is often mixed with cannabis, for making joints or smoking bongs. If you mix cannabis with tobacco you'll be taking on the same risks you get from smoking tobacco.

These are: addiction to nicotine (the drug in tobacco), coughs, chest infections and in the longer-term, cancer and heart disease.

Mixing

Is it dangerous to mix with other drugs?

Yes, any time you mix drugs together you take on new risks.

For example, if you drive when stoned or high you double your chances of having a fatal or serious injury car crash, but if you drive after mixing cannabis with alcohol, you're 16 times more likely to crash.

Smoking or vaping cannabis with tobacco increases the risk of becoming addicted to nicotine which is the addictive drug in tobacco.

Addiction

Can you get addicted?

Yes. Heavy cannabis users often get cravings and find it hard not to take the drug – even when they know it's causing them physical, mental or social problems.

When heavy users do try to stop they can:

- feel moody and irritable
- feel sick
- find it hard to sleep
- find it hard to eat
- experience sweating and shaking
- get diarrhoea

If you roll your spliffs with tobacco, you're also at risk of getting addicted (or staying addicted) to nicotine.

The law

Class: B

This is a Class B drug, which means it's illegal to have for yourself, give away or sell.

Possession can get you up to 5 years in prison, an unlimited fine or both.

Supplying someone else, even your friends, can get you up to 14 years in prison, an unlimited fine or both.

Like drink-driving, driving when high is dangerous and illegal. If you're caught driving under the influence, you may receive a heavy fine, driving ban, or prison sentence.

If the police catch people supplying illegal drugs in a home, club, bar or hostel, they can potentially prosecute the landlord, club owner or any other person concerned in the management of the premises.

Additional law details

Cannabis is different to other Class B drugs as it comes under the discretionary warning scheme.

This means that a police officer can choose to issue you with a street warning only (which doesn't form a criminal record, though it will be recorded), so long as:

- you're in possession of a small amount of cannabis only, and for your personal use
- it's the first time you've been caught with an illicit drug and you have no previous record of offence
- you are compliant, non-aggressive and admit that the cannabis is for your own use only

If you're caught with cannabis and it's your second offence, the police can issue with a fixed-term fee notice, which is an on-the-spot fine for £80.

As long as you pay that within 21 days, there's no criminal record. If there's a third occasion, you will be arrested and taken to the police station.

The above information is reprinted with kind permission from FRANK.
© 2022 FRANK

www.talktofrank.com

Cannabis: the facts

Cannabis (also known as marijuana, weed, pot, dope or grass) is the most widely used illegal drug in the UK.

The effects of cannabis can vary a lot from person to person. It can also vary depending on how much or how often it's taken and what it contains.

Some examples include:

- feeling chilled out, relaxed and happy
- laughing more or become more talkative
- feeling hunger pangs ('the munchies')
- feeling drowsy, tired or lethargic
- feeling faint or sick
- having problems with memory or concentrating
- experiencing mild hallucinations
- feeling confused, anxious or paranoid

Can you get addicted to cannabis?

It's possible to get addicted to cannabis, especially people who are considered regular or heavy users.

If regular users stop taking cannabis, they may get withdrawal symptoms, such as feeling moody and irritable, feeling sick, difficulty sleeping, difficulty eating, sweating, shaking and diarrhoea.

Regularly smoking cannabis with tobacco also increases the risk of becoming addicted to nicotine and experiencing withdrawal symptoms from nicotine as well as cannabis if you cut down or give up.

Regularly using tobacco also increases the risk of tobacco-related diseases such as cancer and coronary heart disease.

Trying to give up cannabis?

If you need support with giving up cannabis:

- see a GP
- visit Frank's Find support page
- call Frank's free drugs helpline on 0300 123 6600

Marijuana Anonymous is a free self-help group. Its '12 step' programme involves stopping using marijuana with the help of regular face-to-face and online support groups. You can call them on 0300 124 0373 (callback service).

Cannabis and mental health

Regular cannabis use increases the risk of developing a psychotic illness, such as schizophrenia.

A psychotic illness is one where you have hallucinations (seeing things that are not really there) and delusions (believing things that are not really true).

The risk of developing a psychotic illness is higher in people who:

issues: Discussing Cannabis

- start using cannabis at a young age
- smoke stronger types, such as skunk
- smoke it regularly
- use it for a long time
- smoke cannabis and also have other risk factors for schizophrenia, such as a family history of the illness

Cannabis also increases the risk of a relapse in people who already have schizophrenia, and it can make psychotic symptoms worse.

Other risks of cannabis

Other risks of regularly using cannabis can include:

- feeling wheezy or out of breath
- developing an uncomfortable or painful cough
- making symptoms of asthma worse in people with asthma
- reduced ability to drive or operate machinery safely

If you drive while under the influence of cannabis, you're more likely to be involved in an accident. This is one reason why drug driving, like drink driving, is illegal.

Cannabis and pregnancy

Cannabis use may affect fertility. Regular or heavy cannabis use has been linked to changes in the female menstrual cycle, and lower sperm count or lower sperm quality in men.

Using cannabis while pregnant may harm the unborn baby. Cannabis smoke contains many of the same harmful chemicals found in cigarette smoke.

Regularly smoking cannabis with tobacco increases the risk of a baby being born small or premature.

Cannabis has not been linked to birth defects, but research suggests that using cannabis regularly during pregnancy could affect a baby's brain development as they get older.

Does cannabis have medicinal benefits?

Cannabis contains active ingredients called cannabinoids. two of these – tetrahydrocannabinol (THC) and cannabidiol (CBD) – are the active ingredients of a prescription drug called Sativex. This is used to relieve the pain of muscle spasms in multiple sclerosis.

Another cannabinoid drug, called Nabilone, is sometimes used to relieve sickness in people having chemotherapy for cancer.

Clinical trials are under way to test cannabis-based drugs for other conditions including cancer pain, the eye disease glaucoma, appetite loss in people with HIV or AIDS, and epilepsy in children.

Read the latest updates on cannabis, cannabinoids and cancer – the evidence so far on the Cancer Research UK website.

3 December 2020

The above information is reprinted with kind permission from the NHS.
© Crown copyright 2022
This information is licensed under the Open Government Licence v3.0
To view this licence, visit http://www.nationalarchives.gov.uk/doc/open-government-licence/

www.nhs.uk

Legalising cannabis will create jobs – and save lives

As the party of entrepreneurship and sound public finances, it's high time the Tories end the 'war on drugs' and decriminalise weed.

By Rachel Cunliffe

The ranks of former ministers who publicly support drug reform are both full and varied.

There's Bob Ainsworth, Tony Blair's health minister, who called for all illicit drugs to be regulated and legally available back in 2010. There's Jacqui Smith, who admitted in 2012 that her decision as Labour home secretary to upgrade cannabis to a Class B drug was wrong. There's the Liberal Democrat former health minister Norman Lamb, who backed the legalisation of possession and consumption of cannabis in 2018.

And most recently, there's Conservative grandee and former leader of the party Lord Hague, who wrote a comment article earlier this month arguing that 'decriminalising drugs is the only way forward'.

What this diverse bunch have in common is that they only found the courage to speak out after they had left office, and were therefore no longer in a position to do anything about it. Convenient for them, as they didn't have to face the political pressure of a public that has been terrified into submission by the US-led 'war on drugs' for the past 50 years – a policy that has caused untold misery and cost many lives.

But over the last two decades, at least, the US has been changing course. Marijuana for medicinal use is legal in 36 states, for recreational use in 18, while trailblazing Oregon has decriminalised personal possession of all drugs. In the UK, in contrast, drug laws have been stuck in a time warp – in defiance of not only the science but the economics and global politics.

The moral case for drug reform is inarguable. Fifty years of prohibition have not led to a decline in addiction and deaths – on the contrary, drug-related deaths in England and Wales hit a record high this year and have been rising for the past eight, while in Scotland they are higher than anywhere in Europe.

A sixth of inmates are in prison for drug offences, to say nothing of those whose crimes are linked to their addiction. The hypocrisy, when multiple members of the Cabinet – including the Prime Minister – have admitted to their own drug use is staggering.

At the same time, while UK law technically changed in 2018 to allow medicinal cannabis in some very specific circumstances, the regulations imposed by an establishment petrified of being considered 'soft' on drugs are so strict that the vast majority of desperate patients – from epileptic children to people battling cancer – cannot access it.

Even politicians who are unsure about fully decriminalising all drugs know our cannabis laws are a disaster. They know it is wrong to condemn someone to a criminal record for

possession of a drug that is less harmful (to the user and to society) than alcohol or tobacco, just like they know sending people to prison, where they are more likely to become dependent on far more harmful drugs than they are on the outside, is fuelling the UK's spiralling addiction crisis. That's why they keep changing their minds once they are no longer in power.

If we are to 'follow the science' and 'save lives', to use our Prime Minister's favoured terms, we need a different way to make the case to the public. And as the party of business, sound finance and entrepreneurship, the Conservatives are the ones to do it.

The first issue is simply one of cost – something any government struggling with the finances of a pandemic should have front of mind.

In 2018 the TaxPayers' Alliance found that legalising cannabis 'could save at least £891.7 million a year in reduced spending by police, prisons, courts and the NHS through pain relief treatments'. For context, that's the amount the March 2020 budget pledged to invest to help British businesses lead the way in high-potential technologies.

Speaking of those high-potential technologies, cannabis could be the new gold rush. The UK is already a world leader in growing medicinal cannabis, which is then exported in the absence of a legal market here. As our European neighbours press ahead with reform Britain risks being left behind on a multibillion-pound industry.

A few years ago the Adam Smith Institute estimated a regulated UK market could be worth £6.8 billion a year, increasing tax revenue by £1.05 billion. In fact, back in 2015 a report by the Treasury itself found similar. That's a much more appealing prospect than the post-pandemic tax rises Rishi Sunak seems fixated on.

The kind of jobs a legal market would bring – in bioscience, agritech, marketing and retail – are either areas where the UK already excels, or where the pandemic destroyed job opportunities. As the furlough scheme winds down next month, imagine if the Conservatives could turn to the hundreds of thousands who have lost their jobs, and offer them a career in a cutting-edge new sector.

You won't hear Labour making these arguments. It is up to the Tories to change the terms of the argument, to talk both about ending the cruelty of the current anti-science approach and of inspiring a new generation of entrepreneurs, saving taxpayers money at the same time.

The late campaigner for drugs reform, and former smuggler, Howard Marks, was fond of pointing out that legal or illegal, cannabis sellers would always make billions – the only madness was gifting all that money solely to organised crime.

Hague's intervention shows it is not un-Conservative to imagine another way forward. It's time for the self-appointed party of both business and law and order to see sense.

30 August 2021

The above information is reprinted with kind permission from *The Telegraph*.
© Telegraph Media Group Limited 2021

www.telegraph.co.uk

Differences between cannabis laws in the US and the UK

By Maja Talevska

British and American cannabis laws are very different, and cannabis use is just one of the many things that highlight this claim. The two countries today have a different approach to the consumption of cannabis and its products, so here are some facts for everyone who wants to know the main differences.

The US states make their own regulations

Even though the United Kingdom and the United States of America can be said to have similar regulations, they act in a different way when it comes to cannabis. Every state in the US makes its own regulations regarding cannabis use.

Before 1973, Texas was one of the US states with harshest laws where possession of any amount of marijuana was classified as a felony. In 1973, Texas started a liberating trend in which a slight change in its law made owning less than four ounces a misdemeanour. After that, several states made similar changes where laws were relaxed, and offences were treated as minor criminal deeds.

Since the turn of the 21st century, scientists have made severe scientific breakthroughs in medical marijuana use. That's when most states decided to change their regulations and make cannabis legal, at least to some point.

Today, according to the marijuana legalisation statistics, medical cannabis is legal in 33 states, while recreational cannabis is legal in 11 states. However, the degree of legalisation is not the same everywhere, and that's the main difference between UK and US laws.

Many US states have been steadily decriminalising cannabis and various types of drug use or possession over the last two decades. The Government's goal has been to ease prison overcrowding and reduce the cost and the social burdens caused by prosecuting minor drug offenses. In California for instance, drug law changes enacted in 2014 caused felony drug crime arrests to plummet 79%.

In the US, every state can create its law and enforce penalties. There are five basic levels of legality. For example, cannabis is fully legal in California. In the state of Ohio, it's legal for medical use, and it's also decriminalised. In Arizona, it's not decriminalised, but it's legal for medical use. Cannabis is legal in Texas for medical use but has a THC level regulation. In Idaho, it's fully illegal.

The UK only allows medical marijuana

The UK has one law for all countries. In 2018, medical marijuana was allowed in Wales, England, and Scotland. However, recreational marijuana is still not allowed.

According to British law, cannabis is considered a Class B drug. In 2004, it was declared a Class C, but it was changed back to Class B in 2009. The difference between these classes is the severity of legal punishment. Also, getting caught with illegal drugs from Class B will get you in more serious trouble because the penalty will be worse.

Thanks to the law passed in 2018, doctors are allowed to prescribe cannabis products. Patients can also buy them over the counter, but the authorities heavily monitor the production and use. That proves that the British government acknowledges the health benefits of marijuana, but it's still not ready to make it legal for recreational use, although the government doesn't mind people taking CBD oil which is legal in the uk.

What's the penalty for getting caught using marijuana?

Recreational marijuana is still illegal in the UK, so getting caught by the police means that you can get fined or prosecuted. If you get caught smoking marijuana for the first time, the police can either confiscate it or let you go with a warning. However, if you get caught again, the fine is £90. Getting caught for the third time means going to jail for 28 days if found guilty.

In the US, laws and legal punishments are different from state to state. Since there are 50 states, that means 50 different regulations. Despite some states declaring cannabis use as fully legal, there are still limitations of some kind. In Colorado, for example, also known as the US capital of marijuana, adults over 21 are allowed to possess up to one ounce of cannabis. People there are also allowed to grow up to six cannabis plants for personal use.

In Idaho, on the other hand, marijuana is illegal for all purposes. People getting caught with less than three ounces will face jail time of up to one year. Getting caught with more may result in five years in prison. All the other states have laws and regulations that are somewhere in between these two states.

Conclusion

Cannabis laws in the UK are not as strict as in some US states. Still, the battle for marijuana legalization is yet to be fought in the country. Medical marijuana was allowed just two years ago, and even though recreational marijuana use is prohibited, it's still not as strict as in some other parts of the world.

1 June 2020

The above information is reprinted with kind permission from The Student Lawyer.
© 2022 The Student Lawyer

www.thestudentlawyer.com

10% of teenagers have tried hard drugs by age 17

Almost a third of 17-year-olds have tried cannabis and one in 10 have tried harder drugs, such as cocaine, ecstasy and ketamine, with similar rates of experimentation regardless of parents' education level, finds a new study by UCL Institute of Education (IOE) researchers.

The research, published today in a briefing paper by the Centre for Longitudinal Studies at the UCL Social Research Institute, examines engagement in substance use and antisocial behaviours among Generation Z as they reached late adolescence.

The researchers analysed new data collected from a nationally representative group of almost 10,000 teenagers who have been taking part in the Millennium Cohort Study (MCS) since they were born in 2000-02. In 2018-19, when study participants were age 17, they were asked about substance use – including drug taking, binge drinking and smoking – and antisocial behaviours – such as assault, shoplifting and vandalism. The researchers were also able to study how substance use and antisocial behaviours develop across adolescence by comparing data at age 17 to data collected from participants at age 14.

The new study revealed that 31% of young people had tried cannabis and 10% had tried harder drugs by age 17. More than half (53%) had engaged in binge drinking – drinking five or more drinks at a time – and 9% said they had done this on 10 or more occasions in the past year. More than two fifths (45%) had tried a cigarette, and 12% were regular smokers at age 17. As expected, for all of these behaviours, rates had increased substantially since participants were age 14.

The authors discovered differences in rates of substance use according to sex, parents' education level and ethnicity.

Males reported higher rates of cannabis use than females (34% vs 28%), harder drug taking (12% vs 8%) and binge drinking (56% vs 51%). Young people whose parents were highly educated – holding at least a degree – were more likely to report having tried alcohol than those whose parents had lower level qualifications (89% vs 82%). They were also more likely to have engaged in binge drinking (59% vs 50%). Rates of drug use remained similar among young people, regardless of parents' educational qualifications.

White teenagers were much more likely to have experimented with substances than their ethnic minority peers. They were

twice as likely to report taking harder drugs (11% vs 5%) and almost three times more likely to report binge drinking than ethnic minority teens (59% vs 21%).

As Generation Z approached adulthood, reports of antisocial behaviours mostly remained stable or declined compared to rates at age 14. Prevalence of assault – pushing, shoving, hitting, slapping or punching someone – decreased from 32% at age 14 to 25% at age 17, and levels of vandalism, graffitiing and use of a weapon were similar at both ages. However, reports of shoplifting increased from 4% in early adolescence to 7% a few years later.

Rates of certain antisocial behaviours differed by sex and parents' education level. Males were almost three times more likely than females to report assaulting someone at age 17 (36% vs 13%). Young people whose parents were educated to degree level or higher reported higher rates of shoplifting than their peers whose parents had lower level qualifications (9% vs 5%). In contrast, prevalence of antisocial behaviours was similar among white teens and their ethnic minority counterparts.

Co-author Professor Emla Fitzsimons (UCL Centre for Longitudinal Studies) said: 'To some extent, experimental and risk-taking behaviours are an expected part of growing up and, for many, will subside in early adulthood. Nevertheless, behaviours in adolescence can be a cause for concern as they can have adverse long-term consequences for individuals' health and wellbeing, and their social and economic outcomes.'

'The prevalence of alcohol consumption in this study is very similar to that found in an English cohort born 12 years before, and which measured alcohol use around the same age. However, reports of cannabis use in our study suggest a decline compared to rates among this earlier born generation. It remains to be seen how the COVID-19 pandemic has affected engagement in these behaviours.'

Co-author Dr Aase Villadsen (UCL Centre for Longitudinal Studies) added: 'In relation to our finding for antisocial behaviours we might have expected to have seen a larger increase from the age of 14 to 17 in line with the well-established age-crime curve shown in previous research, whereby these behaviours worsen over adolescence, and then decline again in late adolescence and early adulthood.

'This surprising finding could show that the peak in antisocial behaviours in this generation has been reached earlier than usual and rates have already started to come down by age 17. Or it may be because young people nowadays are engaging in a much lower level of offending than in the past; official figures have shown plummeting rates of youth offending in the last decade. This is a positive and will potentially help to improve the future social and economic prospects of Generation Z.'

The study was funded by the Economic and Social Research Council (ESRC).

10 February 2021

The above information is reprinted with kind permission from University College London.
© 2022 UCL

www.ucl.ac.uk

Illegal drug use by young people is more than double official estimates, major study reveals

It has led to fears Government data could be hampering efforts to combat drug use.

By Charles Hymas, home affairs editor

Illegal drug use by young people is more than double official estimates, according to a major study amid fears it may be hampering efforts to combat the problem.

The research by Bristol University found more than a third (36.7 per cent) of young people aged 16 to 24 admitted to taking illegal drugs including cannabis, cocaine or amphetamines in the past year.

This compared with just 16.4 per cent in the Office for National Statistics' (ONS) *Crime Survey for England and Wales*, which is used by Government policy makers to develop strategies to combat illegal drugs use.

The researchers believe the reason for the underestimate by the official ONS survey lies in the methodology because the Bristol findings are based on in-depth relationships with families who have been tracked by academics for years.

By contrast, the ONS results are based on one-off, face-to-face interviews where the participants may be more reluctant to admit their illegal drug use to a stranger.

The same disparity was shown in figures for 'lifetime' use of drugs with the ONS estimating just 40.6 per cent of young people up to the age of 24 had taken an illegal drug, and the Bristol figure a full 20 per cent higher at 62.8 per cent, nearly two thirds of the cohort.

The biggest disparity was in cannabis use where the ONS was 23.2 per cent lower, compared with a deficit of 16.9 per cent for cocaine use during their lifetimes up to the age of 24.

The Bristol research, known as *Children of the 90s*, is based on close tracking of 14,000 pregnant women and their children since 1991/92 when they were recruited and followed up every year collecting their biological, environmental and lifestyle data.

Dr Lindsey Hines, Wellcome postdoctoral fellow at Bristol Medical School, a senior author of the study, said: 'The two data sets use very different methodologies to collect the data, which may be a contributing factor to these differences.

'The Crime Survey is a one-off face-to-face survey whereas Children of the 90s has a long-standing relationship of trust with their participants, who have completed postal questionnaires every year since they were teenagers.

'Our study suggests that this trusted relationship, built over decades with participants, could lead to young people reporting their drug use more accurately.

'Reliable measures of illicit drug use are vital for developing effective policy and treatment programmes, and the UK figures come from the *Crime Survey for England and Wales*.'

The researchers also found similar disparities for young people's drinking, where hazardous drinking was double the rate in the Bristol study compared with official surveys.

Where the Bristol research suggested 60.3 per cent reported hazardous drink at age 24, the official figure was 32.1 per cent. There was, however, no difference for tobacco use when the Bristol study was compared with official surveys.

Lead author Hannah Charles, an epidemiology scientist at PHE, said it suggested health officials were underestimating illegal drug use which had implications for measures to support and help young people.

'As *Children of the 90s* participants are drawn from one region of the UK, we urgently need to expand this work to other longitudinal health studies (also known as birth cohort studies) to further validate the results,' she said.

'The nature of and illegality of drug use means it is often a difficult area for researchers to get honest data. We're not saying they are mis-reporting the levels, but rather the methodologies could be complemented by other methods and validated using cohort studies, that could help to build up this trust.'

18 January 2021

The above information is reprinted with kind permission from *The Telegraph*.
© Telegraph Media Group Limited 2021

www.telegraph.co.uk

Cannabis misuse

An extract from the report *Drug misuse in England and Wales: year ending March 2020*.

Since the year ending December 1995, cannabis has consistently been the most-used drug in England and Wales. In the latest year, 7.8% of adults aged 16 to 59 years (around 2.6 million) reported using cannabis in the last year. This is a substantially greater proportion of individuals than the next most prevalent drug, powder cocaine at 2.6% (around 873,000). Cannabis was also the most common drug used by young adults, 18.7% of those aged 16 to 24 years old (around 1.2 million) had reported using the drug in the last year.

There was no change in the prevalence of cannabis use in the last year compared with the previous year. However, there has been a long-term decline compared with year ending December 1995 from 9.5% for adults aged 16 to 59 years and 26% for adults aged 16 to 24 years (see Figure 3).

More recently, cannabis use in the last year has seen small annual increases. Compared with the year ending March 2013, there has been a 1.5 percentage point increase among 16- to 59-year-olds and a five percentage point increase for 16- to 24-year-olds.

Frequency of use

Cannabis was the most common drug used but it also had a significantly greater proportion of frequent users than powder cocaine or ecstasy. Among adults aged 16 to 59 years, around one-third of individuals who used cannabis were frequent users and had used the drug more than once a month in the last year compared with 8.7% of powder cocaine users and 1.9% of ecstasy users. The estimates for 16- to 24-year-olds were similar.

9 December 2020

The above information is reprinted with kind permission from the Office for National Statistics.
© Crown copyright 2021
This information is licensed under the Open Government Licence v3.0
To view this licence, visit http://www.nationalarchives.gov.uk/doc/open-government-licence/ **OGL**

www.ons.gov.uk

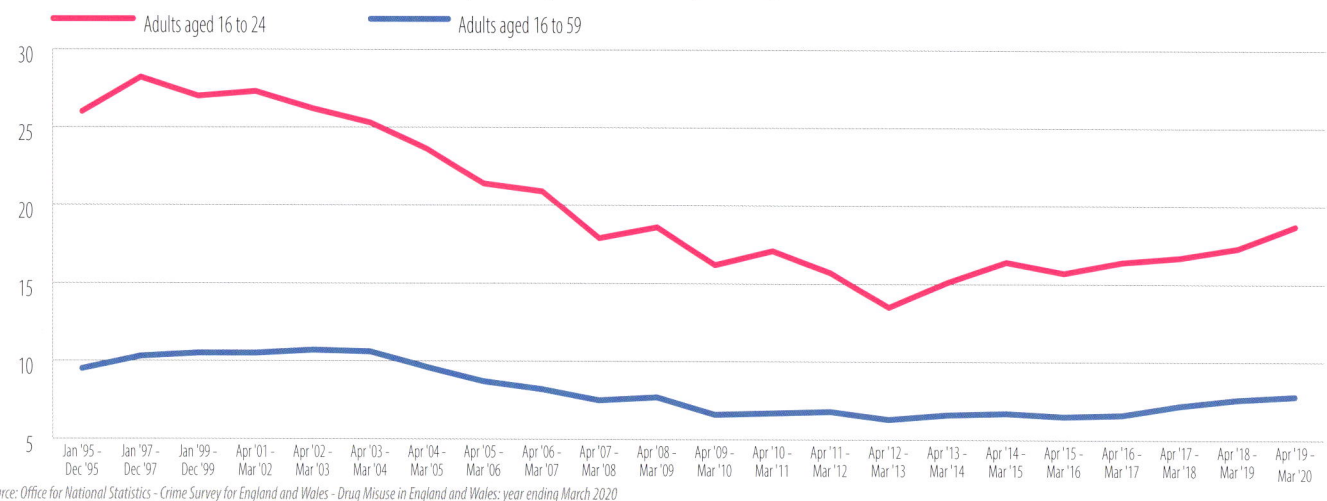

Figure 3: Cannabis use in the last year has increased compared to year ending March 2013
Proportion of adults aged 16 to 59 years and 16 to 24 years reporting use of any drug, any Class A drug and cannabis in the last year, England and Wales, year ending December 1995 to year ending March 2020

Source: Office for National Statistics - Crime Survey for England and Wales - Drug Misuse in England and Wales: year ending March 2020

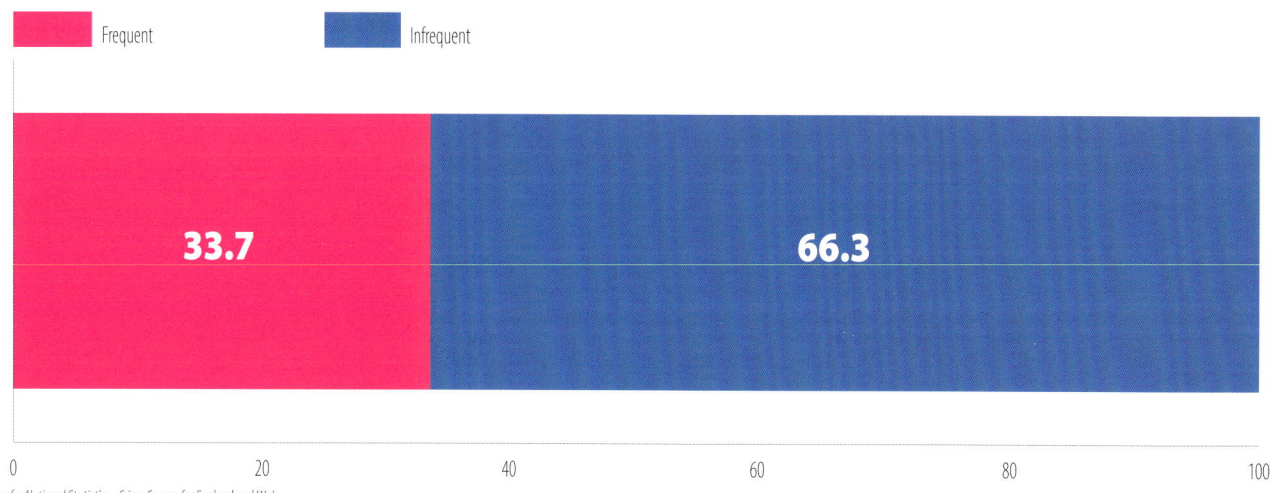

Figure 6: A third of those who used cannabis in the last year were frequent users
Proportion of adults aged 16 to 59 years who had taken cannabis, powder cocaine or ecstasy in the last year by frequency of use, England and Wales, year ending March 2020

Source: Office for National Statistics - Crime Survey for England and Wales

Cannabis strength soars over past half century – new study

Largest study on how cannabis has changed over time finds increased strength putting consumers at greater risk of harm.

New research shows that over the past 50 years street cannabis across the world has become substantially stronger carrying an increased risk of harm.

The team behind the study from the Addiction and Mental Health Group at the University of Bath, synthesised data from over 80,000 cannabis samples tested in the past 50 years from street samples collected in the USA, UK, Netherlands, France, Denmark, Italy and New Zealand. Their findings are published in the journal *Addiction* and the research was funded by the Society for the Study of Addiction.

The researchers investigated how concentrations of THC (the intoxicating component of cannabis responsible for giving users a 'high') had changed over time in different types of cannabis. In herbal cannabis, they found that THC concentrations increased by 14% from 1970 to 2017. This was primarily due to a rising market share of stronger varieties such as sinsemilla relative to traditional herbal cannabis which contains seeds and less THC.

The team have previously found consistent evidence that frequent use of cannabis with higher levels of THC carries an increased risk of problems such as addiction and psychotic disorders.

Lead author Dr Tom Freeman, Director of the Addiction and Mental Health Group at the University of Bath, said: 'As the strength of cannabis has increased, so too has the number of people entering treatment for cannabis use problems. More Europeans are now entering drug treatment because of cannabis than heroin or cocaine.'

The researchers found that the increases in THC were particularly high for cannabis resin, with THC concentrations rising by 24% between 1975 and 2017. Cannabis resin is extracted from herbal cannabis and is now typically stronger than herbal cannabis according to the findings.

They also looked at concentrations of cannabidiol or CBD, which is not intoxicating but may have potential medical uses such as helping people to quit cannabis. In contrast to THC, they found no evidence for changes in CBD in cannabis over time.

Study co-author Sam Craft also from the Addiction and Mental Health Group at the University of Bath explained: 'Cannabis resin - or '"hash" - is often seen as a safer type of cannabis, but our findings show that it is now stronger than herbal cannabis. Traditionally, cannabis resin contained much lower amounts of THC with equal quantities of CBD, however CBD concentrations have remained stable as THC has risen substantially, meaning it is now much more harmful than it was many years ago.'

Cannabis is the most widely used illicit drug in the world but has recently been legalised in Canada, Uruguay and several states in the USA. The findings of this new study have particular relevance in light of growing demands to legalise cannabis in an attempt to make it safer. Most recently a referendum in New Zealand (which ultimately failed to receive public support) included measures to limit the strength of cannabis sold through legalisation.

The researchers argue that increases in cannabis strength highlight the need to implement wider strategies for harm reduction similar to those used for alcohol - such as standard units and public guidelines on safer consumption limits.

Dr Tom Freeman added: 'As the strength of cannabis has risen, consumers are faced with limited information to help them monitor their intake and guide decisions about relative benefits and risks. The introduction of a standard unit system for cannabis – similar to standard alcohol units – could help people to limit their consumption and use it more safely.'

15 November 2020

The above information is reprinted with kind permission from the University of Bath.
© University of Bath 2022

www.bath.ac.uk

Cannabis Use

Chapter 2

The effects of marijuana on your brain and body

Ingesting cannabis triggers a cascade of effects that can influence your bodily function.

Medically reviewed by Dr Roger Henderson and words by Annie Hayes

Cannabis, marijuana, hash, weed… there are a variety of different ways to refer to the leaves, stems and flower buds of the Cannabis sativa plant, which is typically smoked, vaped or consumed in food for its mind-altering effects.

The effects of weed vary from person to person, depending on how it's consumed, how much you use, and how often you use it.

While mostly consumed recreationally – it's the UK's most widely-used illegal drug – medicinal marijuana is also available on prescription for certain medical symptoms and conditions.

The drug can cause both immediate and long-term effects, whether used legally or illegally. Here, pharmacist Navid Sole explains how cannabis interacts with the brain, and talks us through the effects of weed on different parts of the body:

The effects of weed on your brain and body

The most prominent psychoactive compound in cannabis is Tetrahydrocannabinol (THC). It's one of at least 113 cannabinoids identified in cannabis, and is responsible for the feeling of being 'high'. 'THC is shown to affect a specific set of sites in the brain – the hippocampus, cerebellum and the basal ganglia,' says Sole.

Each of these parts of the brain are linked to Endocannabinoid System (EC), which exists and is active in your body, even if you don't use cannabis. Endocannabinoid receptors are an important part of this system, and are found throughout your body. When endocannabinoids – molecules made by your body – bind to them, it signals to the EC that it needs to take action.

Tetrahydrocannabinol (THC) is one of at least 113 cannabinoids identified in cannabis, and is responsible for the feeling of being 'high'.

'When someone smokes marijuana, THC gets into the brain rapidly and attaches to these receptors,' says Sole. 'The EC

issues: Discussing Cannabis

system is finely tuned to react appropriately to incoming information. But THC overwhelms the EC system. It prevents the natural chemicals from doing their job properly and throws the whole system off-balance.'

Research has linked the EC to a variety of bodily functions, from inflammation levels to liver function, metabolism to learning and memory. This is why, when THC binds to these receptors, it triggers a cascade of effects that can influence your bodily function.

Effects of weed on your brain

The most noticeable effects of weed occur due to changes in the brain and central nervous system. When you ingest cannabis, the THC 'triggers your brain to release large amounts of the feel-good hormone, dopamine, making you feel happy,' says Sole. This can heighten your senses – for example, colours might appear brighter, or sounds may seem louder – and also warp your sense of time.

In the hippocampus, which is responsible for your memory, THC changes the way you process information. It can make it harder to focus, learn, and remember things. This also makes it harder to create new memories, Sole says. Typically, these effects only last for 24 hours or so after you stop ingesting cannabis.

However, the drug can harm developing brains. Using cannabis heavily in your teenage years may cause these effects permanently. Similarly, babies whose mothers use cannabis during pregnancy may develop issues with memory and concentration.

Marijuana is thought to temporarily ease chronic pain and inflammation. It has been shown to help control epileptic seizures, and relax stiff muscles and reduce spasms in people with multiple sclerosis. However, it also impairs brain areas that play roles in movement. 'Changes also take place in the cerebellum and basal ganglia, which means that ingesting cannabis can alter your balance, coordination, and reflexes,' says Sole.

Effects of weed on your lungs

The most common way to ingest cannabis is to smoke it, either with tobacco – for which the associated health risks are widely known – or on its own. 'Similar to tobacco, marijuana smoke comprises a variety of toxic chemicals, which are an irritant to your throat and lungs,' says Sole. These include ammonia and hydrogen cyanide, which can cause inflammation.

Cannabis may also damage your immune system, making you more susceptible to other illnesses. 'Those who smoke marijuana regularly will experience wheezing, coughing and produce an increased quantity of phlegm – as well as being at high risk of bronchitis and lung infections,' he continues. Cannabis smoke also contains carcinogens, so it may increase your risk of lung cancer, though research into this is ongoing.

Effects of weed on your blood

When you use cannabis, the THC enters your bloodstream and begins to circulate around your body. This process occurs quickly when you smoke or vape weed, and slowly when you consume it in food – for example, in a brownie. When this occurs, your heart rate speeds up by as much as 20 to 50 beats per minute, says Sole, and can last as long as three hours.

A meta-analysis of the health records of more than 20 million US patients aged 18 to 55 found that those who used cannabis were 26 per cent more likely to have a stroke than those who abstained. They were also 10 per cent more likely to have developed heart failure.

One of the most obvious – and frequently stereotyped – effects of weed are the bloodshot eyes. This is caused by blood vessels in the eyes expanding. But this isn't necessarily a bad thing. In fact, by reducing blood pressure in the eyes, cannabis may temporarily ease symptoms of glaucoma, but research into this is ongoing.

Furthermore, scientists are looking into positive associations between cannabis, the circulatory system, and cancer. Scientists believe the drug may help stop the growth of blood vessels that feed cancerous tumours, however more research is needed before any claims can be made.

Effects of weed on your gut

Cannabis stimulates the appetite, leading to the phenomenon known as 'the munchies'. In some instances, this is a welcome side-effect – for example, it can help people undergoing treatment for AIDS, cancer and other illnesses to regain weight.

Cannabis stimulates the appetite, leading to the phenomenon known as 'the munchies'.

'Marijuana has also been used to ease symptoms of nausea or upset stomach,' says Sole. People who are being treated with chemotherapy are sometimes prescribed cannabis to reduce side effects such as nausea and vomiting. However, when consumed in food, cannabis can cause digestive issues such as nausea and vomiting, due to how it's processed in the liver, Sole adds.

Effects of weed on your mental health

One of the most concerning effects of weed is its implications for mental health issues. While many people use cannabis for its 'mellow' feeling, for some it can bring about the opposite effect, causing agitation, insomnia and irritability. Heavy, prolonged use can cause paranoia and has been associated with mental health disorders, such as depression and anxiety. In high concentrations, THC can cause you to hallucinate or lose touch with reality.

13 October 2020

The above information is reprinted with kind permission from Netdoctor
Courtesy of Hearst Magazines UK
© 2022 Hearst UK

www.netdoctor.co.uk

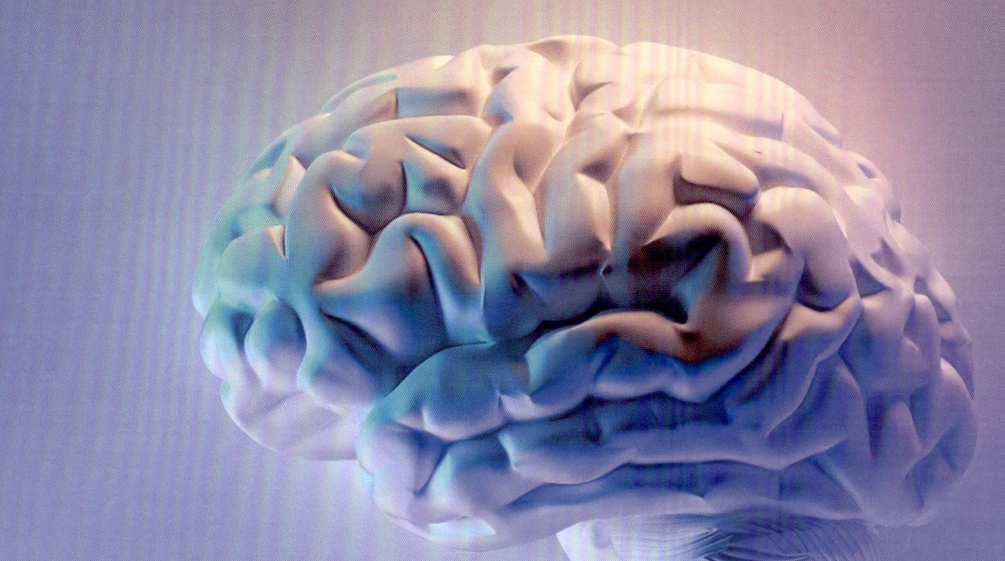

Smoking cannabis just once can change a teenager's brain

Scientists say it could have serious implications.

By Sarah Young

Teenagers who use cannabis just once or twice may end up with changes to the structure of their brain, scientists have warned.

A study, conducted by researchers at Swinburne University of Technology in Melbourne, Australia, found that there were clear differences on brain scans between teens who said they had smoked cannabis a couple of times and those who had never tried it.

Until now, research using animals to study the effects of cannabis on the brain have shown effects at low levels, leading researchers to believe that changes might occur during early stages of cannabis use.

However, the study's lead author, Catherine Orr, says she 'was surprised by the extent of the effects'.

The researchers analysed images from 46 14-year-olds who said they had used marijuana once or twice, as well as images from 46 teens who had never tried it, taking into consideration age, sex, IQ, socioeconomic status and use of alcohol or tobacco.

Upon analysing the teens' brain scans, the researchers found clear differences between the two groups, which they suspected were due to low-level cannabis use.

At this stage, the scientists couldn't prove that marijuana led to the differences seen in the scans and acknowledged that it was possible those who chose to use marijuana had different brain structures to begin with.

To address this, the researchers analysed scans from a third group of teens that had not tried marijuana before they had their brain scans at age 14.

By the age of 16, 69 of the participants said they had used marijuana at least 10 times but their brain scans at age 14 looked no different to the brain scans of other teens who had not taken up cannabis.

This meant there could not be any inborn brain difference that predicts a person would later become a cannabis user.

What's more, the scientists discovered there were widespread increases in the volume of grey matter – which is made up of nerve cell bodies and involved in sensory perception and muscle control - in brain regions among those who had smoked marijuana.

According to the researchers, this kind of alteration to the structure of the brain could have serious implications.

'In our sample of cannabis users, the greater volumes in the affected parts of the brain were associated with reductions in psychomotor sped and perceptual reasoning and with increased levels of anxiety two years later,' Orr said.

However, the higher volume of grey matter in cannabinoid-rich regions of the brain could be related to a normal process called 'pruning' which may go awry when teens use marijuana.

As young brains develop, unnecessary or defective neurons are pruned away, Orr explained. But, when the system doesn't work correctly, those cells remain in place.

With rates of cannabis use among adolescents increasing – it's the most frequently used drug in Europe – concurrent with changes in the legal status of marijuana and societal attitudes regarding its use, the scientists believe the new findings are a step forward in understanding the impact it can have on developing brains, but accept that more research needs to be done.

16 January 2019

The above information is reprinted with kind permission from *The Independent*.
© independent.co.uk 2022

www.independent.co.uk

Are weed hangovers real? Expert reveals all

By Dr Peter McCann

It's a common belief that, unlike alcohol, weed is hangover-free

This derives from the belief that alcohol can be a more harmful intoxicant than weed (also known as cannabis or marijuana). As pioneers in leading treatments for cannabis addiction, we know this is not the case.

How does marijuana cause a hangover?

If you smoke cannabis, you will know of the foggy sort of mornings after late-night smoking and know of the residual effects you feel the next day.

The more you smoke weed, the longer it will stay in your system – heavy users often test positive a month or longer after use. And, as long as pot's active ingredient is present in your system, you will be partly under the influence of drugs.

What does a marijuana hangover actually feel like?

- Feelings of sluggishness
- General haziness and fog / scattered mind
- Slow reactions / not feeling so awake
- Waking up feeling confused
- Some report headaches

Weed makes you angry

After using marijuana or having to go without a smoke do you experience an angry outburst? Have your friends ever told you to relax or chill?

Whilst recreational marijuana use is connected to feeling relaxed, many users actually report feeling irritable, short-tempered and even rage after smoking or eating edibles. These symptoms are also more prevalent during withdrawal.

Cannabis addiction

It might be difficult to believe that you might have a cannabis addiction, but if you smoke every day or are a habitual smoker, then you are likely to have an addiction.

For some smoking weed might feel harmless, however, those who have certain traits or have a family history of mood disorders or psychosis should proceed with extra caution.

Ask yourself the following questions:

1. Do you smoke weed daily or near-daily?
2. Do you experience cravings for weed?
3. How much time is dedicated to sourcing, buying and smoking?
4. Has your consumption increased over time?
5. Do you use more than you originally intended?
6. Do you continue to use despite the negative consequences?

If you have answered yes to the above, or spend a considerable amount of time and money purchasing weed on a weekly basis then it is likely you have an addiction.

Cannabis might sound funny to some people, but it is very serious, often leading to mental health conditions and disorders like increased anxiety and depression.

Scientific studies into the effects

An early study on the hangover effects of marijuana found that the effects were different to the acute effects of marijuana, commenting: 'These apparent findings suggest that marijuana smoking can produce residual (hangover) effects the day after smoking.'

What's more telling is that the marijuana used in the study was only 2.9% THC, which is much less potent than the weed on the market today, which is anywhere between 10% and 30%.

So, if such little THC can affect your sense the morning after, then imagine what higher concentrations can do in the same time frame – there's just more to process and metabolize.

What marijuana leaves behind

THC the psychoactive compound which gets you high, is actually a fat-soluble chemical that the body can store for days. And simple movements or exercises can release this THC back into the bloodstream long after consumption.

It's important to note that regular smokers are known to have near-constant levels of THC in their system, which might explain why habitual smokers can exhibit symptoms of depression as activity levels decrease and interest in hobbies, social situations or work.

7 September 2021

The above information is reprinted with kind permission from Castle Craig.
© 2022 Castle Craig

www.castlecraig.co.uk

How does smoking marijuana affect academic performance? Two researchers explain how it can alter more than just moods

An article from *The Conversation*.

By Jason R. Kilmer, Associate Professor of Psychiatry & Behavioural Sciences, School of Medicine, University of Washington & Christine M. Lee, Research Professor of Psychiatry and Behavioural Sciences, School of Medicine, University of Washington

In a trend that coincided with the pandemic, marijuana use among college students in 2020 reached levels not seen since the 1980s. That's according to the latest research from Monitoring the Future – an annual survey that looks at drug and alcohol use among the nation's young people. Below, Jason R. Kilmer and Christine M. Lee – both University of Washington School of Medicine researchers who study marijuana use among college students – explain some of the reasons behind the trend, and some of its consequences.

Why is marijuana so popular among college students as of late?

Research has consistently shown that people report using marijuana in order to feel the high, experience enhanced feelings, increase social connections or cope with certain feelings and moods.

Among young adults early in the pandemic, there were modest reductions in motivations for using marijuana for celebratory reasons and slight increases toward using marijuana because of boredom, possibly due to initial physical distancing mandates and stay-at-home orders. However, among the main reasons for using, both before the pandemic and during as well, are feelings of enjoyment or the high associated with marijuana use.

We do not yet know the impact of these shifting motivations for using marijuana or whether patterns seen during the pandemic will continue after.

How many college students are actually using cannabis?

With 18 states legalizing cannabis for non-medical or 'recreational' purposes – the first of which did so in 2012

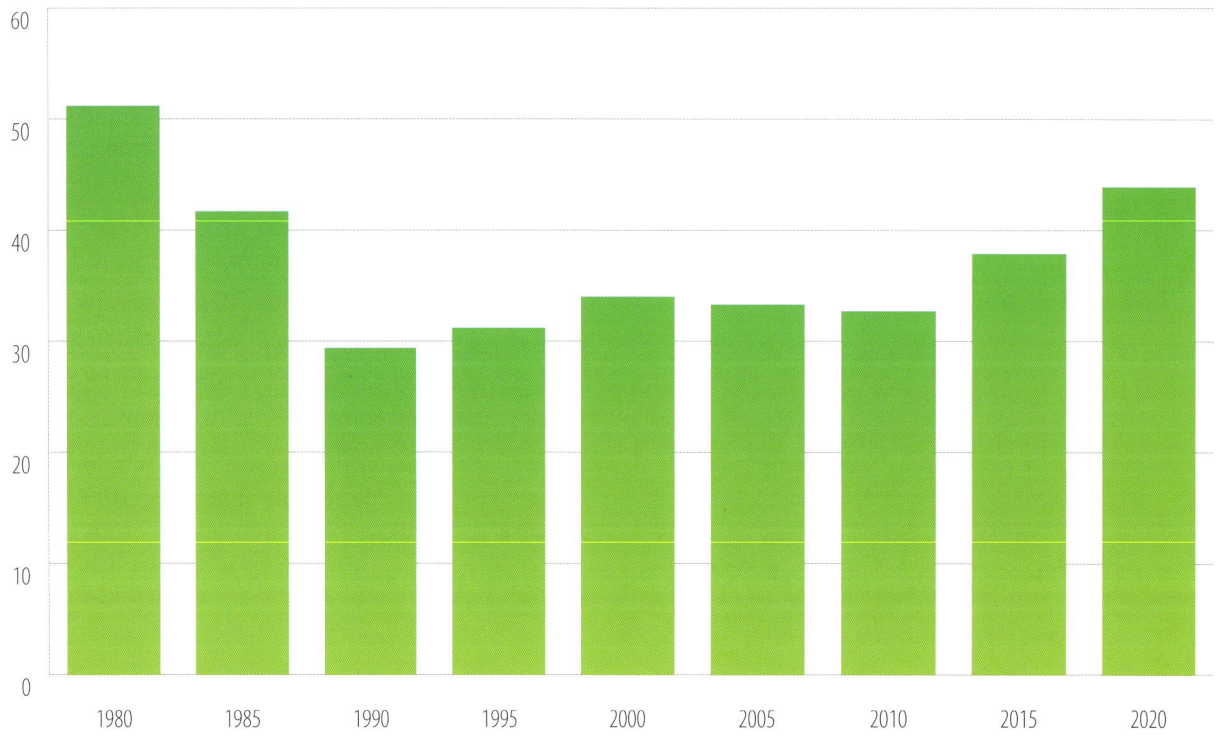

More U.S. college students are consuming marijuana

Since 1980, the percentage of U.S. college students that have consumed marijuana in the past year has fallen, but recent years have seen a rise.

Source: Monitoring the Future

– access to marijuana has increased, especially for college students over 21 years of age. While the past three reports from *Monitoring the Future* – a national drug use survey conducted annually by the University of Michigan – have shown that between 43% and 44% of college students report any cannabis use in the past year, over half of college students do not report use. This is important to note because research has shown that when people think 'everyone' is doing something, they are more likely to start doing it themselves or do it more.

Different from any use in the past year, researchers often look at past month use as an indicator of current use. Given that about 25% of college students report use in the past month, this suggests that three-quarters of students do not report past month use, and not using marijuana is actually the most common behaviour.

How does smoking weed affect academic performance?

As researchers who work with college students, we hear students say things like marijuana is 'safe,' 'natural' or that it's 'just weed,' but research tells a very different story about potential risks. This is particularly true with the high potency cannabis that dominates markets in legal and medical states.

Published research consistently shows that the more frequently a college student uses cannabis, the lower their GPA tends to be, the more they report skipping class and the longer it takes them to graduate.

Probably the most direct impact to academic performance is a relationship between marijuana use and impaired attention and memory. This relationship has been documented for years, including with college students.

The good news is that studies that follow people as they abstain show that when marijuana use stops, cognitive performance improves, though it can take 28 days of abstinence. So much of this depends on how often someone uses and the type or potency of marijuana they are using. But whatever the case, it certainly seems that the more frequently people use, the more likely they are to experience challenges with attention, memory and other cognitive abilities.

In an August 2021 article about recommended guidelines for lower-risk cannabis use, the authors concluded that people who use cannabis and experience impaired cognitive performance should think about taking a break or significantly reducing how much they use, or the potency of what they use.

Are there any academic or educational benefits?

In our conversations with college students, we hear some students who typically use marijuana say that when they don't use, they can't sit still, or they feel restless and anxious. These students might assume that marijuana use is 'helping' them.

Unfortunately, the anxiety and restlessness they experience when not using marijuana can be symptoms of withdrawal. Those things could also be indicative of addiction to cannabis, or what is called a cannabis use disorder. This might mean when students continue to use marijuana, they might feel a sense of less anxiety or restlessness, but are actually making withdrawal symptoms stop by resuming use.

We are not aware of any studies that point to academic or educational benefits of using marijuana.

Are we forgetting anything?

Science has to play catch-up on the cannabis products being sold today. Among the many cannabinoids in cannabis, THC, the psychoactive component typically associated with the 'high' from marijuana, is arguably the most well studied. In the U.S., THC concentrations in the 1970s on average were under 2%, reached 3% in the 1980s, were 4% by the mid-1990s and steadily climbed to almost 15% by 2018.

Today, especially in legal markets, we are seeing even higher concentrations. For example, in Washington state, flower products – that is, marijuana that is smoked – commonly exceed 20% THC. Concentrates, which include dabs, hash oil and other products, routinely exceed 60% THC.

'High potency' cannabis is considered to be anything over 10% THC. Use of high potency cannabis is associated with a number of outcomes, including greater risk of cannabis use disorder and adverse mental health outcomes.

Young people seem to be particularly vulnerable. Although we sometimes hear from people that marijuana use doesn't seem that risky, recent studies make clear that cannabis use may increase harms and risks for those who use. For college students, these issues range from having trouble concentrating and paying attention to feeling antisocial or paranoid.

13 October 2021

The above information is reprinted with kind permission from The Conversation.
© 2010-2022, The Conversation Trust (UK) Limited

www.theconversation.com

Mental health and cannabis

What is cannabis?

Cannabis is an illegal drug that is made from a group of plants; Cannabis sativa, Cannabis indica, and Cannabis ruderalis. Cannabis plants have psychoactive properties, and people use it for different reasons, such as to relieve mental or physical problems. However, although benefits may be felt initially, in the longer term it can make problems worse, or create new ones. Cannabis use is risky as it affects different people in different ways and no one can tell what their reaction may be.

Cannabis is the most widely used illegal drug in the UK, and young people are more likely to use it than older people. Unfortunately, consuming cannabis at a young age is thought by scientists to adversely affect the brain, and lead to things such as issues with memory and learning, and poor mental health.

How does it work?

Tetrahydrocannabinol (THC) is the main psychoactive chemical in cannabis. The more THC in cannabis, the stronger the effects will be. THC is responsible for the 'high' feeling that some people experience. Once it enters your bloodstream, the THC can affect you in just a few minutes, and last up to a couple of hours. THC floods the brain with dopamine, known as the 'feel-good' chemical. However, researchers believe that there is evidence to show that long-term exposure to THC actually leads to a decrease in levels of dopamine. This means that long-term users are more likely have a blunted dopamine response, and so will be less likely to experience the 'highs' that they felt when first taking the drug.

THC is also known to affect the hippocampus, the part of the brain that is responsible for creating memories. This has the effect of memory-loss.

How can cannabis make me feel?

The effects that cannabis has can vary, depending on how much or how often it used, what it contains, and down to the person taking it. Not everyone will feel the same way, and its impossible to tell if it will make you feel good or bad each time you take it.

Some of the effects that cannabis can have on you are:

- feeling chilled out
- feeling relaxed and happy
- laughing more or become more talkative
- having 'the munchies' (increased appetite)
- experiencing things around you, such as sights and sounds, more intensely
- having an altered perception of time or events
- feeling drowsy, tired or lethargic
- feeling sick
- feeling faint
- having problems with memory and/ or concentrating
- experiencing hallucinations
- feeling confused, anxious or paranoid
- problems with coordination

- delayed reaction time
- increased heart rate
- decreased blood pressure
- lower inhibitions, which may lead to dangerous behaviour or situations.

As you can see, most effects are not very nice, and you run the risk of experiencing one or many of these if you take cannabis.

Is cannabis addictive?

Evidence suggests so. About one in ten people can become addicted to cannabis, meaning that they become dependent to their use of the drug, even if it is negatively affecting their everyday life. For teens, the risk is increased to about one in six, but for some people it could be even higher than this.

One of the other risks of cannabis use, is that of the withdrawal symptoms that you may experience when trying to stop using it. From effects that can be mental or physical, symptoms of withdrawal can include:

- depression
- anxiety
- restlessness
- irritability
- difficulty sleeping
- problems with your stomach
- sweating or chills
- headaches

If you use cannabis regularly, the brain starts to depend on the supply of THC. When you stop taking it, the brain and body have to adjust, and so the withdrawal symptoms start. As you can see from the list above, withdrawal can be extremely unpleasant.

How can cannabis affect my mental health?

According to research, people who start using cannabis in their teens tend to have more memory and learning problems than those who don't use cannabis. However, it is not clear if these effects are permanent.

People who start using cannabis in their teens may also have a higher risk for mental health issues later in life, including schizophrenia. But experts still aren't sure how strong the link between the two is.

Regular use can increase the risk of developing a psychotic illness. Psychosis is when you have an alternate or distorted sense of reality, which can include hallucinations (seeing or hearing things that are not real) or delusions (believing things are not true). These can be incredibly scary and distressing.

Schizophrenia is a psychotic illness that can develop after using cannabis. However, its not really clear if drug use is the cause, or if people who develop schizophrenia are more likely to use drugs. It is clear though, that cannabis use can make psychotic conditions much worse, as you're more likely to experience the negative side effects.

1 February 2022

Cannabis users at 'much higher' risk of developing poor mental health

Those with a recorded history of cannabis use in general practice records are at a much higher risk of developing mental ill health problems such as anxiety or depression as well as severe mental illnesses, new research shows.

The findings point to the need for a public health approach to the management of people misusing cannabis, including the need to emphasise the importance of general practitioners to continue enquiring about recreational drug use.

While the links between cannabis use and severe mental illnesses such as schizophrenia and psychosis are well researched, the associations are less clear between cannabis use as described in patients' GP records and other, more common types of mental ill health such as depression and anxiety.

In a new study, published in *Psychological Medicine*, researchers in the University of Birmingham's Institute for Mental Health and the Institute of Applied Health Research found a strong link between general practice recorded cannabis use and mental ill health in one of the largest cohorts ever explored.

Senior author Dr Clara Humpston said: 'Cannabis is often considered to be one of the "safer" drugs and has also shown promise in medical therapies, leading to calls for it be legalised globally. Although we are unable to establish a direct causal relationship, our findings suggest we should continue to exercise caution since the notion of cannabis being a safe drug may well be mistaken.'

Dr Joht Singh Chandan said: 'The research reaffirms the need to ensure a public health approach to recreational drug use continues to be adopted across the UK. We must continue to progress measures to improve the prevention and detection of drug use as well as implement the appropriate supportive measures in an equitable manner to prevent the secondary negative health consequences.'

Using primary care data drawn from the IQVIA Medical Research Database (IMRD-UK), the researchers found following the first recorded use of cannabis, patients were three times more likely to develop common mental health problems such as depression and anxiety. In addition, they were almost 7 times more likely to develop severe mental illnesses such as psychosis or schizophrenia.

The dataset included records from 787 GP practices around the UK gathered over a 23-year period between 1995 and 2018. The researchers were able to include data from 28,218 patients who had a recorded exposure to cannabis. These were matched to 56,208 patients who had not been using cannabis and controlled for sex, age, ethnicity, smoking status and other relevant characteristics.

The cannabis users also had much higher rates of having a recorded history of using other drugs such as heroin, cocaine and amphetamines.

Future research in this area will investigate the levels of cannabis use or the potency of ingredients.

1 October 2021

The above information is reprinted with kind permission from the University of Birmingham.
© University of Birmingham 2022

www.birmingham.ac.uk

Cannabis users five times more likely to have suicidal thoughts, study finds

People who smoke marijuana every day are most at risk, with female smokers particularly susceptible.

By Joe Pinkstone

Cannabis users are up to five times more likely to have suicidal thoughts than non-smokers, a new study shows.

The class B drug has long been anecdotally linked with mental health problems, including depression and anxiety.

But a study of more than a quarter of a million young adults in the US, run by the National Institutes of Health, assessed the strength of the connection.

It revealed that around 3 per cent of the population who do not smoke cannabis and do not suffer from depressive episodes have some suicidal thoughts.

But the prevalence of suicidal thoughts increased the more often a person smoked a joint.

For example, seven per cent of people who smoked cannabis, but less than once a day, reported suicidal thoughts, rising to nine per cent for those who smoked the drug every day.

But 14 per cent of people with a diagnosed cannabis use disorder, who often smoked the drug several times a day, reported suicidal feelings, a five-fold increase compared to non-smokers.

The figures were higher for people who already suffered from depression with one in three (35 per cent) non-smokers with the mental illness having thoughts pertaining to suicide.

Cannabis use disorder

This already elevated baseline figure then rises further to 44 per cent in those who use cannabis, to 53 per cent of those who use cannabis daily, and to 50 per cent in people with 'cannabis use disorder'.

'While we cannot establish that cannabis use caused the increased suicidality we observed in this study, these associations warrant further research, especially given the great burden of suicide on young adults,' said Dr Nora Volkow, senior author of the study from the National Institute on Drug Abuse (NIDA) in Maryland.

'As we better understand the relationship between cannabis use, depression, and suicidality, clinicians will be able to provide better guidance and care to patients.'

The researchers also looked at how smoking marijuana impacted men and women differently, and discovered female users were more prone to problematic thoughts.

Data show that around one in seven (13.9 per cent) women who have no track record of depression but have a cannabis use disorder have suicidal leanings. However, this figure is just 9.9 per cent for men.

Among individuals with both cannabis use disorder and major depressive episodes, the amount of people with suicidal thoughts was 52 per cent higher for women (23.7 per cent) than men (15.6 per cent).

'Suicide is a leading cause of death among young adults in the United States, and the findings of this study offer important information that may help us reduce this risk,' explained lead author Dr Beth Han, from NIDA.

'Depression and cannabis use disorder are treatable conditions, and cannabis use can be modified.

'Through better understanding the associations of different risk factors for suicidality, we hope to offer new targets for prevention and intervention in individuals that we know may be at high risk.

'These findings also underscore the importance of tailoring interventions in a way that take sex and gender into account.'

Suicide was the cause of 5,619 deaths in England and Wales in 2019 and 4,303 of these were men, according to data from the Office for National Statistics.

Men aged between 45 and 49 experienced the highest number of suicides, accounting for 25.5 deaths per 100,000 males.

Figures from 2020, a year ravaged by the coronavirus pandemic, have not yet been released due to the long delay in collecting suicide statistics.

But despite initial concern the lockdowns would see an increase in suicides, preliminary data indicates 2020 is likely no worse than 2019.

The findings of the new study are published in the medical journal JAMA Network Open.

22 June 2021

The above information is reprinted with kind permission from *The Telegraph*.
© Telegraph Media Group Limited 2021

www.telegraph.co.uk

How does cannabis use affect sleep duration?

Recent cannabis use has been shown to affect extremes of nightly sleep duration, being either less than six hours or more than nine hours, with more intense patterns among heavier users.

Published online in the journal *Regional Anesthesia & Pain Medicine*, a study of a large representative sample of US adults revealed a pattern of sleep duration when using cannabis.

Showing more sleep duration extremes among heavier users – those using on 20 out of preceding 30 days – the study suggests that cannabinoids may have therapeutic value for pain relief, and possibly anxiety and sleep disorders as well.

Cannabis use in North America is increasing, with around 45 million adults in the U.S using it in 2019, which is double the figure reported in the early 2000s. This increase is partially due to the widespread decriminalisation of cannabis in many states over the past decade.

Only two thirds of Americans get the recommended 7-9 hours of sleep every night, and almost half report daytime sleepiness every day. Cannabis has therefore also become a popular sleeping aid, especially since sleep deprivation and insomnia continues to increase.

85% of medical cannabis users say the drug helps sleep

Current evidence on the impact of cannabis on the sleep-wake cycle has been unclear, so researchers wanted to see if cannabis use might be linked to nightly sleep duration in a nationally representative sample of US adults, aged 20-59, who had taken part in the biennial National Health and Nutrition Examination Survey (NHANES) from 2005 to 2018.

Researchers asked if respondents reported difficulty falling asleep, staying asleep, or slept too much in the preceding 2 weeks, as well as whether they had ever consulted a doctor about a sleep problem, and whether they regularly experienced daytime sleepiness on at least 5 of the preceding 30 days.

Survey respondents were characterised as recent or non-users depending on whether they had or hadn't used cannabis in the past 30 days.

Sleep duration was defined as:
- short – less than 6 hours
- optimal – around 6 to 9 hours
- long – more than 9 hours

Data was collected on potential influential factors such as age, race, educational attainment, weekly working hours, a history of high blood pressure, diabetes, and coronary artery disease, weight in BMI, smoking, heavy alcohol use – 4 or more drinks daily – and prescriptions for insomnia-aiding opioids, and stimulants.

25,348 people responded to the surveys between 2005 and 2018, but the final evaluation is based on only 21,729 respondents who answered all the questions, representing an estimated 146.5 million US adults.

The average nightly sleep duration was discovered to be slightly less than 7 hours across the sample. Around 12% reported less than 6 hours sleep, while 4% reported more than 9 hours nightly.

A total of 3132, or 14.5% of the respondents said they had used cannabis in the preceding 30 days. They were 34% more likely to report short sleep and 56% more likely to report long sleep than those who hadn't used cannabis in the preceding 30 days.

And they were also 31% more likely to report difficulty falling asleep, staying asleep, or sleeping too much in the preceding 2 weeks, and 29% more likely to have discussed a sleeping problem with a doctor. But recent cannabis use wasn't associated with frequent daytime sleepiness.

Recent users were more likely to report extremes in sleep duration

The analysis looking at the frequency of cannabis use revealed that moderate users – defined as using on fewer than 20 out of the past 30 days – were 47% more likely to sleep 9 or more hours a night compared with non-users.

Heavy users – using cannabis on 20 or more out of the preceding 30 days – were 64% more likely to experience short sleep, and 76% more likely to experience long sleep compared with non-users.

The responses to the study varied across the survey years, and the study's limitations included the reliance on self-reported data and the lack of information on cannabis dose. This study may have also been affected by the stigma associated with cannabis use, which may prompt respondents to lie on the study questions.

Researchers said: 'Increasing prevalence of both cannabis use and sleep deprivation in the population is a potential cause for concern. Despite the current literature demonstrating mixed effects of cannabis and various cannabinoid formulations on sleep architecture and quality, these agents are being increasingly used as both prescribed and unprescribed experimental therapies for sleep disturbances.

'Our findings highlight the need to further characterize the sleep health of regular cannabis users in the population… Sleep-wake physiology and regulation is complex and research about related endocannabinoid pathways is in its early stages.'

7 December 2021

The above information is reprinted with kind permission from Open Access Government.
© 2022 Adjacent Digital Politics LTD

www.openaccessgovernment.org

Cannabis triggered my derealisation disorder

Doing weed is meant to help you relax, but sometimes it can do exactly the opposite. Stewart was 18 when he first started smoking skunk. He tells The Mix about his experience of derealisation and how it triggered his anxiety disorder.

By Nishika Melwani

My experience of derealisation disorder

The first time I experienced derealisation was the most frightened I've ever been in my life. It happened during my first year at uni after smoking some very strong skunk. I was fine at first; I remember laughing with my friends, then suddenly I was having a weed panic attack and everything became confused. It felt as if my soul had drifted out of my body.

I knew I was still alive, but I didn't feel like I was sharing the same reality as everyone else. The way I felt didn't match what I was seeing. I was sure that I had done irreversible damage to my brain. In the following days and months friends persuaded me that I would feel normal again, but three months passed and the derealisation symptoms were getting stronger and stranger. My relationships and work started to suffer.

Seeking help for my derealisation symptoms

It was Christmas and I was at home with my family. I was in the bath and the feeling of being detached were so intense that I believed I might disappear altogether. My emotions felt completely different from my rational observations. I wanted to cry but I couldn't because, as I found out later, a common experience with my condition is the inhibition of 'emotional colouring' and depth. That night I finally broke and told my parents what I was going through. They were shocked and angry at first, but supported me hugely over the coming years.

Over the next two years I tried desperately to find out what was happening to me. First I saw a counsellor, but he just seemed baffled by my problems. Next I asked my doctor (GP) to refer me to a specialist in brain damage and had a brain scan but the results came back as normal. Meanwhile, I was trying deep tissue massage, mineral deficiency testing, hypnotherapy and cranial osteopathy, but none of it worked. I felt so helpless; I was certain that I would never feel right again.

Struggling to be understood

In my second year, life got even harder. It was difficult to leave the house because my symptoms were made worse by busy or new situations. I would rarely go out to pubs or clubs. My close friends tried to understand what I was going through, but they couldn't. I had to turn down evenings out, holidays and time bonding with them. The loss of my sense of humour and mental agility made me feel like I was boring to be around and a burden to everyone.

When I went home to see my parents I spent a lot of time lying in my room in the dark. My parents found it really hard to see their son wasting his youth and engaging so little with life.

Recovery

Recovery began in as extreme a way as my condition had started. The stress, confusion and misery finally culminated in an almighty, spiralling panic attack; one of the worst episodes of depersonalisation I'd had. I rang for an emergency GP to visit my home. With his consent, I admitted myself into a psychiatric unit for monitoring. I arrived at the hospital at 2am, was checked in and given heavy doses of Valium.

When I saw the head psychiatric doctor three days later, he explained to me that in his opinion I had precipitated an anxiety/stress disorder with the use of a powerful form of marijuana. The strange feelings of disassociation and related symptoms were a result of anxiety levels reaching such high levels that my mind was unable to cope with all the adrenaline and cut itself off from reality, causing what is known as derealisation disorder and depersonalisation disorder. These are both a type of dissociative disorders where the person feels detached from their body and their surroundings.

Getting a diagnosis

So, finally I realised that I didn't have a personality disorder or anything like that, my derealisation symptoms were simply the product of a traumatic event. He put me on a drug for the anxiety and over a period of about two months I gradually returned to my former self. My sense of humour and mental faculties came back and I began to reconnect with my emotions.

Five years on and I'm still on meds. I only experience derealisation and anxiety during periods of stress or change now, and I'm learning to cope with the disorder much better. I find that keeping busy and spending time with people you trust is a great distraction. As long as you don't indulge your depression or anxiety and have a strong support network, anyone with psychiatric disorders can live a full life.

27 August 2021

The above information is reprinted with kind permission from The Mix.
© 2022 The Mix

www.themix.org.uk

Cannabis-impaired driving: here's what we know about the risks of weed behind the wheel

An article from *The Conversation*.

By Dina Gaid, Post-doctoral fellow, School of Pharmacy, Memorial University of Newfoundland, Jennifer Donnan, Assistant Professor, School of Pharmacy, Memorial University of Newfoundland, Lisa Bishop, Associate professor, School of Pharmacy, Memorial University of Newfoundland, Maisam Najafizada, Assistant Professor of Population Health Policy, Memorial University of Newfoundland, Maria Josey, PharmD Student, School of Pharmacy, Memorial University of Newfoundland, Michael Blackwood, MSc Student, School of Pharmacy, Memorial University of Newfoundland

Cannabis is the second-most widely used substance in Canada, after alcohol. While there is an in-depth understanding of the impact of alcohol on driving, cannabis is a much more complex substance and can affect consumers differently depending on the product type, amount used and a person's potential tolerance.

This has led to a number of misconceptions about the true impact of cannabis on driving. Research has shown that Canadians perceive driving under the influence of cannabis to be less risky than alcohol, and that they are also less likely to intervene when others engage in such behaviours.

Our Cannabis Health Policy and Research Partnership (CHERP) research team spoke to 91 youth and young adults over the summer of 2021 to get their perspective. They indicated that driving under the influence of cannabis was normalized behaviour, and because it was not believed to be as risky, there was peer pressure to drive after cannabis use.

In fact, driving under the influence of cannabis can be a very risky behaviour, which is a grave public health concern. It is essential to provide education and promote public awareness.

Driving under the influence of cannabis

A recent study has shown that the legalization of cannabis has not increased the rate of traffic accidents or injuries resulting from driving under the influence of cannabis. Care must be taken to not misinterpret this as cannabis being safe.

A 2012 analysis summarizing nine earlier studies on cannabis and driving showed that cannabis doubled the risk of a fatal or serious injury crash. Cannabis-impaired driving was associated with four to 12 per cent of all injuries and mortalities from motor vehicle accidents in Canada in 2012. The reality is that Canadians have been engaging in risky driving behaviours even before cannabis was legal.

A *Statistics Canada* report showed that in 2019, 13.2 per cent of cannabis consumers with a valid driver's licence reported driving within two hours of consuming cannabis. This rate was unchanged from the 2018 pre-legalization report.

Cannabis impairment of driving behaviours

Driving measure	Cannabis effect
Steering instability	No effect
Increase steering wheel reversals/variability	No effect
Excessive speed or slowness	No effect
Speed variablity on curves, decreased cornering stability	Impaired
Increases braking distance/stop time	Impaired
Increased lateral position errors	Impaired
Errors in speedometer tracking	Impaired
Altered passing behaviour	Impaired
Increased start time (in respose to light signal)	Impaired

Source: Pearlson, Stevens, D'Souza 2021 DOI: 10.3389/fpsyt.2021.689444), Author provided

Another study, conducted by Public Safety Canada in 2017, reported even higher rates of cannabis-impaired driving, with 28 per cent of those who consumed cannabis indicating that they had operated a vehicle impaired.

Cannabis impairs driving differently than alcohol

Driving needs full concentration, and making the right decisions at the right time can save lives. Cannabis containing tetrahydrocannabinol (THC) affects motor co-ordination and reaction time, can cause hallucination and increases the risk of getting into a collision. Many studies show strong evidence that cannabis use negatively affects performance on driving-related cognitive tests on a variety of driving tasks.

The idea that cannabis is less risky than alcohol may stem from the fact that impairment from cannabis can differ from alcohol. The biggest difference being that with cannabis, consumers are less aware of their level of impairment.

Alcohol consists of a single chemical that has been well studied for decades. It has a reliable test that measures blood alcohol levels and those blood alcohol levels match to levels of impairment. Cannabis on the other hand consists of several chemicals that lead to varying levels of impairment.

THC is the chemical we know the most about and the one that leads to the greatest impairment from cannabis. However, other less studied chemicals may also impair driving, and we are only at the beginning stages of learning about these effects. There are roadside tests to detect levels of THC in the blood, but the relationship between those levels and impairment is not as clear as those with alcohol.

Factors that affect impairment

It is difficult to predict the exact effect cannabis will have on a particular individual. Impairment can be based on many factors, including the dose of THC, personal experience with cannabis, individual biology and the route of consumption (for example, inhaling versus edibles).

There are several types of cannabis products on the Canadian market, and each product has a different amount of THC and takes a varying amount of time to reach its full effects. The following outlines typical time to effect and duration of impairment.

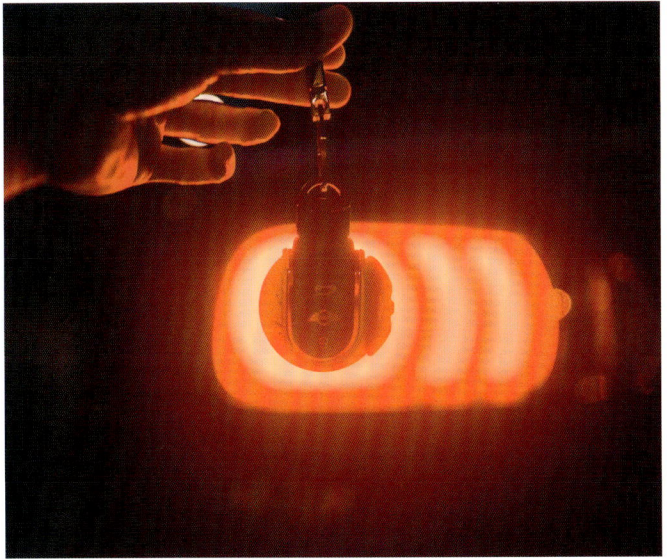

- Inhaling (smoking or vaping): Effects start in about 10 minutes and typically last two to four hours (up to 24 hours)
- Edibles: Effects start in about one hour and typically last four to six hours (up to 24 hours)

Experts recommend waiting a minimum of four to six hours after consuming cannabis containing THC. The combination of cannabis and alcohol intensifies the level of impairment beyond what a user might expect, should always be avoided if driving.

Safety considerations when driving

Cannabis-impaired driving is very risky. It is difficult to advise exactly how long someone should wait after consuming cannabis before driving. The safest choice is to separate cannabis consumption from driving entirely.

However, there are several strategies to avoid this risky situation, including:

- Making sure you have a designated driver,
- Calling a friend or loved one to pick you up,
- Taking public transit,
- Calling a cab or a ride-sharing service, or
- Staying over.

Detection of cannabis-impaired driving

Many young people believe that it is difficult for police to detect and charge drivers who consume cannabis. However, signs of intoxication (bloodshot eyes, smell of cannabis, shallow breathing or rapid heart rate) can form a reasonable suspicion for police. In addition, there are three tests of the Standardized Field Sobriety Tests (SFST) (horizontal gaze nystagmus (involuntary eye movements), one-leg stand and walk and turn) that are performed to evaluate impairment.

In Canada, the Criminal Code prohibits driving while impaired. Penalties range from a minimum fine to imprisonment, depending on the severity of the offence. Impaired drivers who cause injury or death can face longer periods of incarceration, including imprisonment for life.

Information for parents

A Health Canada survey showed that very few parents (11 per cent) said they had discussed the risks of driving under the influence with their teenagers. However, only four per cent of teens indicated they had discussed impaired driving with their parents.

It is essential to start a conversation with children and teens about the risks of driving under the influence of cannabis. Our CHERP research team's public engagement events and social media (Twitter and Facebook) can provide information and resources. Young people need to be prepared to make informed decisions long before they are ready to get behind the wheel.

10 January 2022

The above information is reprinted with kind permission from The Conversation.
© 2010-2022, The Conversation Trust (UK) Limited

www.theconversation.com

Cannabis: increased schizophrenia risk in young people linked to both low and high use

An article from *The Conversation*.

By Ian Hamilton, Associate Professor of Addiction, University of York & Mark Monaghan, Reader in Criminology and Social Policy, University of Birmingham

An estimated 200 million people use cannabis across the world. Next to alcohol and tobacco, it's the most widely used drug in many countries. But while many may no longer see cannabis as a risky or harmful substance, there are still many things experts don't know about cannabis – including why some people develop schizophrenia after use.

Researchers have been investigating the connection between cannabis use and schizophrenia since the late 1960s. Since then, research has confirmed a link between cannabis use and greater risk of developing schizophrenia.

Until now, most evidence has suggested that any link between cannabis and developing schizophrenia is due to using it frequently and at high dosages or that genetic predisposition may be a factor – as might a family history of schizophrenia. But a recent systematic review now shows there's no difference in the risk of developing schizophrenia between both high and low frequency cannabis users.

Frequency of use

To better understand whether or not frequent cannabis use increases risk of adolescents developing schizophrenia, the researchers looked at all material published on the topic between 2010 and 2020 – including studies which previous reviews on the subject had failed to include. They focused on research which looked at adolescents aged between 12 and 18 years old.

They found that both high and low frequency cannabis users were six times more likely to develop schizophrenia compared to those who had never used cannabis. Low use was defined as twice weekly or less, while high use was defined as daily or nearly daily use.

But while they were able to confirm the link between any cannabis use and schizophrenia, there are still some important limitations of this study to note. One of these is the way low and high frequency cannabis use is defined. The definition varies between studies – even those the review looked at – making comparisons difficult.

And as with other drugs, cannabis also varies in potency – and the stronger it is, the greater the risk of a person developing problems, such as schizophrenia, even if their use isn't very frequent. This is not something the review took into account.

Many unknowns

But while we can clearly see there's an association between cannabis use and schizophrenia in young people, we still can't actually be sure that cannabis causes it.

Adolescence and early adulthood are the most common periods during which people develop schizophrenia. Although it can occur at any age, on average it tends to happen in the late teens and early 20s for men, and late 20s and early 30s for women. Adolescence is also a time when many young people begin to experiment with drugs – including cannabis. This makes it very difficult to clearly see whether or not cannabis use actually causes young people to develop schizophrenia.

Some research has also suggested that people who have a greater genetic predisposition to developing schizophrenia may also be more likely to use cannabis. But again, this study still can't definitively show us that cannabis use causes schizophrenia – just that the two are linked.

The other problem we have is that we're unable to predict in advance which people who use cannabis will also develop schizophrenia. This makes public health messaging difficult since we can't specifically target information to those who are most at risk of developing schizophrenia from cannabis use. One estimate even suggests we'd need to prevent 10,500 young people from using cannabis to prevent one case of schizophrenia – further showing how ineffective any public health strategy would likely be. Young people may also not want heed to such warnings, especially if they've already had a positive experience with cannabis. People may also not want to listen to public health warnings about the potential risks because we don't yet know if cannabis use really is causing schizophrenia.

The incidence of schizophrenia in the general population is around one in 300 people – while those who use cannabis have at least a threefold greater risk of developing schizophrenia, making this approximately a one-in-a-hundred risk. While we still can't be absolutely sure that cannabis causes schizophrenia, we can clearly see that use carries a greater risk. And, this latest study shows us that both low frequency and heavy cannabis use carry the same risk.

While perceptions of cannabis's safety have changed in recent years – especially with many countries legalising it for use – it's still important that people think carefully about their risks before using cannabis. This may be especially true for young people who may already be experiencing early signs of mental health problems, as cannabis could worsen these.

25 January 2022

The above information is reprinted with kind permission from The Conversation.
© 2010-2022, The Conversation Trust (UK) Limited

www.theconversation.com

$13 billion US cannabis production industry 'damaging environment', study finds

Researchers found heating, ventilation and air conditioning systems used the most electricity when growing plants.

By Brendan McFadden, Freelance reporter and late editor

The $13 billion US cannabis production industry is creating a huge carbon footprint and damaging the environment, according to new research.

A team from Colorado State University have put together the most detailed analysis of the industry's carbon footprint by assessing indoor cannabis operations across the US where 51 states have legalised cannabis for either recreational or medical use.

Researchers analysed how much greenhouse gas emissions were emitted through the process of growing a cannabis plant – examining how much energy and materials were required to grow the product.

Their study found indoor cannabis production in the country was putting the most strain on the environment, with greenhouse gas emissions found to be between 2,283 and 5,184 kilograms of carbon dioxide per kilogram of dried flower.

Hailey Summers, a graduate who led the study published in Nature Sustainability, said: 'We knew the emissions were going to be large, but because they hadn't been fully quantified previously, we identified this as a big research opportunity space.'

The team found greenhouse gas emissions from cannabis production are largely attributed to electricity production and natural gas consumption from indoor environmental controls.

They also believe emissions are also as a result of high-intensity grow lights supplies of carbon dioxide for accelerated plant growth.

Researchers found heating, ventilation and air conditioning systems used the most electricity when growing plants, with figures varying depending on the area, such as Florida, which requires excessive dehumidifying of plants, or Colorado, where heating is more important.

The high energy consumption of cannabis is due in part to how the product is regulated, according to the team.

In Colorado, many grow operations are required to be in close proximity to retail storefronts, causing an explosion of energy-hungry indoor warehouses in urban areas like Denver.

According to a report from the Denver Department of Public Health and Environment, electricity use from cannabis cultivation and other products grew from 1% to 4% of Denver's total electricity consumption between 2013 and 2018.

The publishing of the findings comes after *New Frontier Data 2018 Cannabis Energy Report* recorded emissions from electricity use in outdoor cannabis growth is 22.7 kilogram per dried flower.

The report, which only examined electricity, found there was 326.6 kilograms of carbon dioxide created per dried flower in outdoor cannabis growth.

8 March 2021

The above information is reprinted with kind permission from *iNews*.
© 2022 Associated Newspapers Limited.

www.inews.co.uk

Chapter 3: Cannabis as Medicine?

Is medical cannabis really a magic bullet?

Research increasingly suggests that extracts from the plant are effective in treating pain, anxiety, epilepsy and more, but experts still preach caution around recreational use.

By David Cox

In 2017, Mikael Sodergren, a liver and pancreatic cancer surgeon at Imperial College Healthcare NHS trust, was finding himself becoming increasingly interested in the potential role of medical cannabis in treating pain, especially the discomfort experienced by patients after complex operations.

'I hope that I do a lot of good, but unfortunately in the short term, I inflict a lot of pain with cancer surgery,' says Sodergren. 'So we're reliant on pretty nasty painkillers, such as high-strength intravenous opioids, which we're trying to move away from. They slow patients down and they cause complications.'

Sodergren was far from alone. Over the past 15 years, an increasing number of scientists have become interested in the potential benefits of medical cannabis for treating all kinds of illness, from multiple sclerosis to anxiety, sleep disorders and post-traumatic stress disorder.

The reason is that phytocannabinoids – chemicals that occur naturally in the cannabis plant – bind to receptors on the body's endocannabinoid system, a complex cell-signalling network stretching throughout the whole body, which is involved in neurological functions ranging from pain-sensing to regulating the sleep-wake cycle.

The phytocannabinoid that has received the most attention of all is CBD. This has become of interest to pain researchers such as Sodergren, because some studies have suggested it might be capable of desensitising pain neurons connected to the endocannabinoid system, while it has been shown repeatedly to have anti-inflammatory effects, which can help reduce seizures in those with childhood epilepsy.

However, medical cannabis is a highly complex and at times contentious field, because it is not just one drug. In total, there are more than 400 different phytocannabinoids in the cannabis plant and while some treatments consist solely of CBD, others utilise the whole plant extract, while the more controversial treatments blend varying concentrations of CBD and tetrahydrocannabinol (THC), the psychoactive element of cannabis, which elicits the 'high' experienced by recreational users. While some studies have suggested that THC might be effective at enhancing the effects of CBD, it has also been linked with an increased risk of psychosis.

'There are several concerns that scientists and medical professionals have with medical cannabis,' says Susan Weiss, director of the Division of Extramural Research at the National Institute on Drug Abuse, in the United States. 'While cannabis is purported to have many benefits, very few indications have rigorous evidence around both the risks and benefits for medical use. Most major safety concerns are related to THC products, but there are also some safety concerns around the use of CBD products. The main safety concerns involve the use of a smoked product, which can lead to a chronic cough and bronchitis, and risks for certain populations such as those with a family history of schizophrenia or psychosis.'

The data on the safety and efficacy of medical cannabis has been fragmented as patients access these products in so many different ways. While laws were changed in November 2018, allowing medical cannabis to be legally prescribed in the UK for the first time, the National Institute for Health and Care Excellence (Nice) has only licensed three CBD-based treatments for use on the NHS. These are available only for three rare types of childhood epilepsy, the vomiting and nausea associated with chemotherapy and multiple sclerosis-related spasticity.

It has been estimated that up to 1.4 million people in the UK are using cannabis for medical purposes, but while some of these individuals are being prescribed products by private GPs and pharmacies, others are buying CBD oils of different concentrations from health food shops or the whole plant extract from recreational dealers.

To try to get a fuller picture of how different forms of cannabis are potentially benefiting patients, private clinics around the globe have begun creating dedicated medical-cannabis registers. These are collating as much data as possible on the types of cannabis being used by different patient groups, on what has proved effective and on any potential safety issues. In the coming years, they hope that this could persuade Nice, and regulators around the world, to improve access to medical cannabis for more conditions.

Data collection

In December 2019, Sodergren established the UK Medical Cannabis Registry, to follow patients who have been prescribed various medical cannabis products by clinicians at the private Sapphire Medical Clinics practice for a range of different ailments.

In May 2021, results were released for the first 129 patients. These showed significant improvements in anxiety, pain and sleep-quality measurements after one and three months. Intriguingly in the context of pain, the treatments appeared to be better tolerated than conventional opioids.

Similar registers are being run by the non-profit research organisation Drug Science, while the Cannabis Care clinic in Auckland, New Zealand, has been following 253 patients on CBD-based treatments. They also demonstrated improvements in quality of life for people suffering from chronic pain and social anxiety.

Sodergren is hopeful that the accumulation of such data could lead to medical cannabis being regarded as a mainstream method of treating different types of pain in coming years. 'It's coming,' he says. 'I think in five to 10 years we're going to have an NHS-licensed drug for pain. I think there are other conditions such as anxiety and insomnia for which the evidence is going to build quickly and we'll have licensed medicines.'

However, others feel that in the absence of rigorously conducted randomised controlled trials, the evidence base remains sparse, especially for complex conditions such as anxiety. Because the UK Medical Cannabis Registry data covers a range of different forms of medical cannabis, some say that it does not help with the tricky question of working out the best formulation and dose to use for a particular disease.

'The main issue we have is that medical cannabis use is still very poorly defined,' says Marta Di Forti, a psychiatrist at King's College London. 'When you look at the data out there, you don't just have medicinal cannabis under one umbrella, you have different substances, taken at different doses, and sometimes combined with other medications and sometimes on their own. Because of this, when I have patients who want to buy CBD over the counter and try it, my recommendation is that they start with the lowest recommended dose and monitor if they experience any adverse side-effects, because we still know so little.'

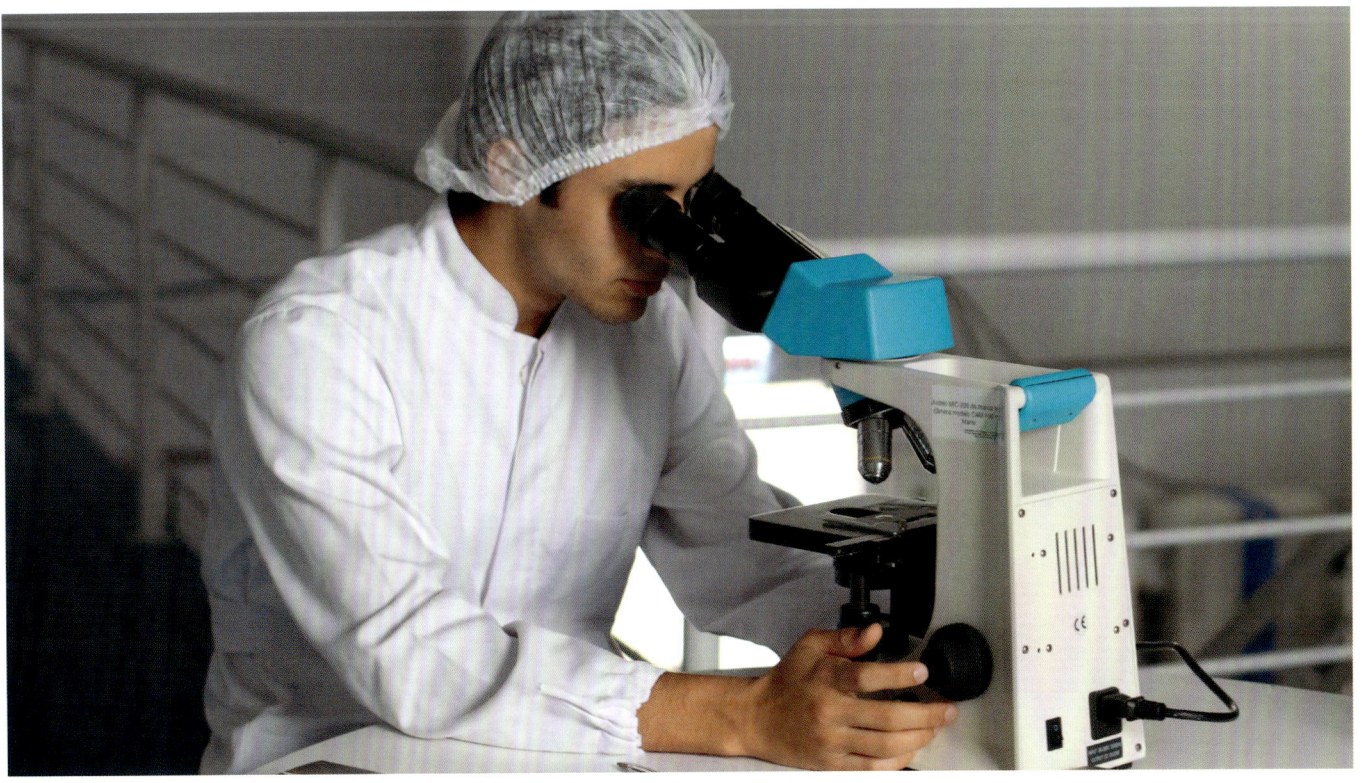

The scientific consensus is that, in the near future, CBD-based medical cannabis is likely to become more widely available as a treatment for different forms of epilepsy, because of its known anti-seizure effects. The CBD-based medication Epidyolex is already licensed by Nice to treat three rare childhood epilepsies and experts in the field predict that it will eventually become available for more common childhood epilepsies and even adult epilepsy as well.

'Because of the success of CBD in controlling seizures in children with these rare, life-threatening conditions, so they go from hundreds of seizures a day to becoming nearly seizure-free, lots of clinical trials are continuing into using CBD for other forms of epilepsy,' says Gary Stephens, a professor of pharmacology at the University of Reading, who was involved in the development of Epidyolex. 'That research is very much ongoing at the moment, but the initial findings look good and I strongly suspect in the next few years that we will be giving CBD for a range of epilepsies. But we need to do big clinical trials to prove that it's better than the placebo.'

Recreational lobbies

Some scientists are concerned about how the growing interest in medical cannabis has been linked to organisations aiming to open up parallel and lucrative recreational markets for the drug. Last year, an investigation by the *British Medical Journal* uncovered connections between organisations researching the use of medical cannabis, such as Drug Science and the Centre for Medicinal Cannabis, with companies lobbying for wider access to recreational cannabis in order to cash in on a great, green windfall.

The potential rewards are obvious. According to Prohibition Partners, a marketing consultancy with a stated mission to open up the international cannabis industry, the entire UK cannabis market could be worth $1.7 billion by 2024, if recreational use is also legalised in the next three years.

But not everyone is comfortable with the recreational and medical cannabis industries being entwined. 'Wherever there is a financial interest, and we don't have enough information scientifically to counterbalance the push for this product, I become very worried as a clinician,' says Di Forti. 'We've seen this in the past with tobacco, which was once advertised as a way to reduce anxiety. I don't want to see history repeating itself.'

Cannabis researchers say that some of the safety concerns over medical cannabis have been overblown, as they are based on data from recreational users, who are often consuming higher and more unregulated doses of the drug. 'Cannabis containing THC is still highly stigmatised unfortunately,' says Anne Schlag, head of research at Drug Science. 'Some of the issues associated with recreational use are not always applicable to medical use.'

Sodergren is keen to distance the debate about whether recreational cannabis should be legalised with research into the medical applications.

'The recreational perspective is really unhelpful to the development of medical cannabis in the UK,' he says. 'What the academic medical profession needs is five to 10 years to tease out the indications what it's going to be useful for and to really understand where these medicines fit in our treatment of illnesses. Having this parallel debate about recreational cannabis just isn't helpful to that process at all.'

For scientists such as Stephens, the way forward is to focus on medical cannabis products that do not contain THC, in order more clearly to separate the medicinal element of these treatments from the recreational side.

'The reason why scientists started studying CBD is because it's non-THC, so we can avoid the stigma,' he says. 'When people first started using medicinal cannabis in the US, there was a big backlash, particularly when it came to use in children. People would come out and say, "How can you get your kids stoned?" Getting Epidiolyx, a CBD-based medicine, into the clinic has helped with that. We're not giving them anything that gets them euphoric, we're giving them something useful and now more research is going on into CBD for other kinds of illnesses.

24 July 2021

The above information is reprinted with kind permission from *The Guardian* & *The Observer*.
© 2022 Guardian News and Media Limited

www.theguardian.com

Medicinal cannabis: what is it and is it legal in the UK?

The law on medicinal cannabis changed in the UK in November 2018.

By Sabrina Barr

Charlotte Caldwell, the mother of 15-year-old Billy Caldwell, has brought her legal campaign to acquire medicinal cannabis for him through the NHS to an end.

Mrs Caldwell and her son made headlines in 2018 when officials at London's Heathrow airport confiscated cannabis-based medicine from them, which had been obtained in Canada to treat his epilepsy.

Billy has refractory epilepsy, which can cause him to have a hundred seizures a day.

The following year, the family launched a legal challenge against the NHS and the department of health in Northern Ireland over access to his cannabis-based medicine.

According to the *Belfast News Letter*, the legal proceedings were withdrawn at Belfast's High Court on Monday 7 September 2020.

The Honourable Mrs Justice Keegan stated: 'There will not be a need for further litigation, which is the last thing this family needs.'

Barrister Monye Anyadike-Danes QC, who represents Mrs Caldwell, added: 'My client thinks this matter can best be pursued through the RESCAS [Refractory Epilepsy Specialist Clinical Advisory Service] panel.'

The RESCAS panel, which is led by Great Ormond Street Hospital, was created in order to bring together paediatric neurologists who specialise in epilepsy, to support patients by offering their expertise.

Mrs Caldwell will now correspond directly with the health professionals on the panel to discuss her son's access to treatment, urging them to ensure her son's prescription is funded, the *News Letter* said.

Speaking on BBC's *The Emma Barnett Show* on Monday 7 September, Mrs Caldwell said that over the past 18 months, she and Billy have been through a 'very, very torturous ordeal', with her son being 'left high and dry by the powers that be'.

She explained that Billy was referred to the RESCAS panel in July this year, with the panel of eminent UK doctors coming to the conclusion 'that there are no legal or clinical barriers to medical cannabis access for Billy'.

So what is medicinal cannabis, what conditions is it used to treat and is it legal to prescribe in the UK?

What is medicinal cannabis and is it legal in the UK?

The term 'medicinal cannabis' is used to refer to any form of medication that contains cannabis, the NHS states.

In the UK, cannabis is classed as a Class B drug.

If a person is found in possession of cannabis, they could face up to five years in prison and/or a fine, according to the government.

If they are found to be supplying and producing the drug, they could face a life sentence, in addition to an unlimited fine.

Medicinal cannabis, on the other hand, is legal in the UK.

On 11 October 2018, the government announced that from 1 November 2018, expert doctors would be given the authority 'to legally issue prescriptions for cannabis-based medicines when they agree that their patients could benefit from this treatment'.

The government emphasised that only a 'specialist doctor' – and not a GP – can prescribe 'these unlicensed medicines'.

'They must make decisions on prescribing cannabis-based products for medicinal use on a case-by-case basis, and only when the patient has an unmet special clinical need that cannot be met by licensed products.'

If a product – such as CBD oil or hemp oil – is marketed as being a form of medicinal cannabis, there is 'no guarantee these are of food quality or provide any health benefits', the NHS states, explaining that these products can be bought legally as food supplements.

CBD is a non-psychoactive chemical compound found in the marijuana plant.

Products that contain CBD (cannabidiol) are not illegal in the UK, as long as they only contain trace amounts of THC (tetrahydrocannabinol), the main psychoactive compound in cannabis.

What conditions is it used to treat?

As explained by the government, while medicinal cannabis is legal, it can only be prescribed by specialist doctors on a case-by-case basis.

In England, only patients with certain health conditions are likely to be prescribed medicinal cannabis, the NHS says.

These include: children and adults who have rare, severe forms of epilepsy; adults who have undergone chemotherapy, which has caused them to vomit or suffer from nausea; and patients with multiple sclerosis whose health condition has caused them to experience muscle stiffness and spasms.

'It would only be considered when other treatments were not suitable or had not helped,' the NHS adds.

The health service states that the 'risks of using cannabis products containing THC (the chemical that gets you high) are not currently clear', which is why further clinical trials are needed.

However, the majority of cannabis products are likely to 'contain a certain amount of THC', the NHS explains.

Side effects of medicinal cannabis can include a decreased appetite, dizziness, fatigue, diarrhoea and nausea.

7 September 2020

The above information is reprinted with kind permission from *The Independent*.
© independent.co.uk 2022

www.independent.co.uk

Legal cannabis: why only 18 people have been given a prescription in the UK despite the law changing

Health Secretary told parents of severely ill children NHS prescriptions would be available in months – a year later many are still waiting.

By Paul Gallagher, Health Correspondent

When Joanne Griffiths met Matt Hancock last March, the Health Secretary told her it would be a matter of months before the cannabis-based medication she is desperately seeking for her severely epileptic son would be available.

Almost a year on Ms Griffiths is still waiting – and she is not alone. When the previous Government announced that patients could be prescribed medicinal cannabis by specialist doctors from 1 November 2018 thousands of parents breathed a sigh of relief. Such products, obtained illegally or from abroad, were making an enormous difference to their children's lives.

Yet as *i* revealed in November, just 18 NHS prescriptions had been issued since the change in the law. Unsurprisingly, Mr Hancock was asked on BBC Breakfast on Wednesday whether he had been lying to Ms Griffiths.

'No, I met her and many other parents whose children benefit from these cannabis-based drugs. I changed the law to allow the cannabis-based drugs to be used in this country,' he answered.

'There was then a report from the National Institute which decides what is paid for on the NHS that came out exactly as she said a few months after our meeting and that report said that the costs that are being charged by the companies are too high.

'Since then I've been working incredibly hard to try to get these drugs available on the NHS… I've been trying to move it forward but it's moved more slowly than I hoped for. I totally understand the efforts of the parents. We've got to keep trying to make progress on this. But it comes down to the drug companies to make them in the right way. They need to come to the table on this.'

Drug companies are only part of the problem, however. The NHS is still dragging its feet on being able to help families fund the cost of cannabis-based treatments.

NHS England's website even admits that 'very few people in England are likely to get a prescription for medical cannabis'.

Availability

Currently, medicinal cannabis is only likely to be prescribed for the following conditions: epidyolex for children and adults with epilepsy, nabilone for chemotherapy patients, and nabiximols (sativex) for people with multiple sclerosis (MS).

Children like Alfie Dingley and Billy Caldwell, whose parents are still fighting for wider access to the new drugs, need the medicine to try to have a normal life – yet still face barriers.

Only specialist doctors in hospitals are allowed to prescribe medicinal cannabis – GPs are not allowed – and many have been reluctant to do so, forcing parents to turn to private doctors and raise the cash themselves.

Several families have accused Boris Johnson and Mr Hancock of betraying them and breaking promises to help them. They are going to No. 10 to hand in a petition calling for wider access to medicinal cannabis on the NHS and will meet MPs in Parliament to try and force action. Some of the families are even considering taking legal action against individual NHS trusts to push through change.

At Prime Minister's Questions in the Commons today, Labour's Ruth Jones asked when medicinal cannabis will be available for the families that need it. All the Prime Minister would say is that it was his government that legalised medicinal cannabis and that Mr Hancock will meet the families.

The families themselves cannot afford to wait any longer. Change needs to happen now.

5 February 2020

The above information is reprinted with kind permission from *iNews*.
© 2022 Associated Newspapers Limited

www.inews.co.uk

Medicinal cannabis campaigners 'closely linked' with recreational supporters

Key figure in Billy Caldwell case also involved with group which lobbies for legalisation of marijuana for recreational use.

By Paul Gallagher, Health Correspondent

Groups campaigning for wider access to cannabis for medical reasons and those pushing for the legalisation of cannabis for recreational use are closely linked, an investigation has uncovered.

By 2024, the UK's medicinal cannabis market is predicted to be worth nearly £1.1 billion, while the recreational market is estimated to be around £1.44 billion.

The *BMJ* investigation highlights the high profile case of Billy Caldwell, a boy with severe epilepsy, who made headlines after his mother Charlotte flew to Canada to get cannabis oil for her son, which was seized at customs on her return.

Steve Moore, former CEO of David Cameron's Big Society initiative, helped to organise Charlotte Caldwell's trip and promote her cause. But Mr Moore's interest in cannabis is not limited to the drug's medicinal use, according to the *BMJ*.

Law change

Mr Moore is strategic counsel for the Centre for Medicinal Cannabis, an industry body for businesses and investors in cannabis medicinal products, and co-founder and strategic counsel of Volteface, an advocacy group set up in 2017 to lobby for legalisation of cannabis for recreational use. He is also strategic counsel for another trade body, the Centre for Medicinal Cannabis, whose members include the Canadian based Supreme Cannabis Company, which has invested in several cannabis brands in Canada and Europe.

Mr Moore declined to comment on whether his engagement with the Caldwell case was part of a conscious effort to normalise the conversation around cannabis, in keeping with Volteface's agenda to see the recreational use of cannabis decriminalised.

But he told the *BMJ*: 'Decriminalisation in and of itself would not financially benefit any legal licensed cannabis companies and there is little indication that the government is considering any such reform.'

Ian Gilmore, director of the Liverpool Centre for Alcohol Research and chair of Alcohol Health Alliance UK, said: 'We must not drift into the situation we found ourselves in with tobacco and alcohol, where global companies seeking to maximise their markets distorted the arguments, often through third parties. We must protect patients from having groups with conflicts of interest building up unrealistic hopes.'

18 March 2020

The above information is reprinted with kind permission from *iNews*.
© 2022 Associated Newspapers Limited

www.inews.co.uk

How many people have tried cannabis-extract products?

Nearly one-in-ten Britons already use products with legal cannabis extracts, and large sections of the population are considering it

By Connor Ibbetson, Data Journalist

Cannabidiol, also known as CBD, is an extract of the cannabis plant - and an increasingly popular ingredient in medicines and cosmetics.

Many other extracts from the same plant are criminalised in the UK, but CBD is completely legal - provided it's obtained from an EU-approved strain.

CBD remains controversial though, with many preaching its health benefits and medicinal properties, despite only a small amount of scientific evidence on the compound's effects.

Britons are certainly curious. A quarter (28%) say they would consider using products containing CBD, although just shy of half (47%) of Britons say they wouldn't touch them.

The products are more popular with younger Britons aged between 18 and 24 years old, with a third (36%) considering trying them. One in ten younger Britons (10%) have already used them, compared to 5% of Britons aged 65 or over.

The most popular type of CBD products with Britons is pure oil (58%), followed by CBD vape juice or e-cigarettes (21%) and creams (11%).

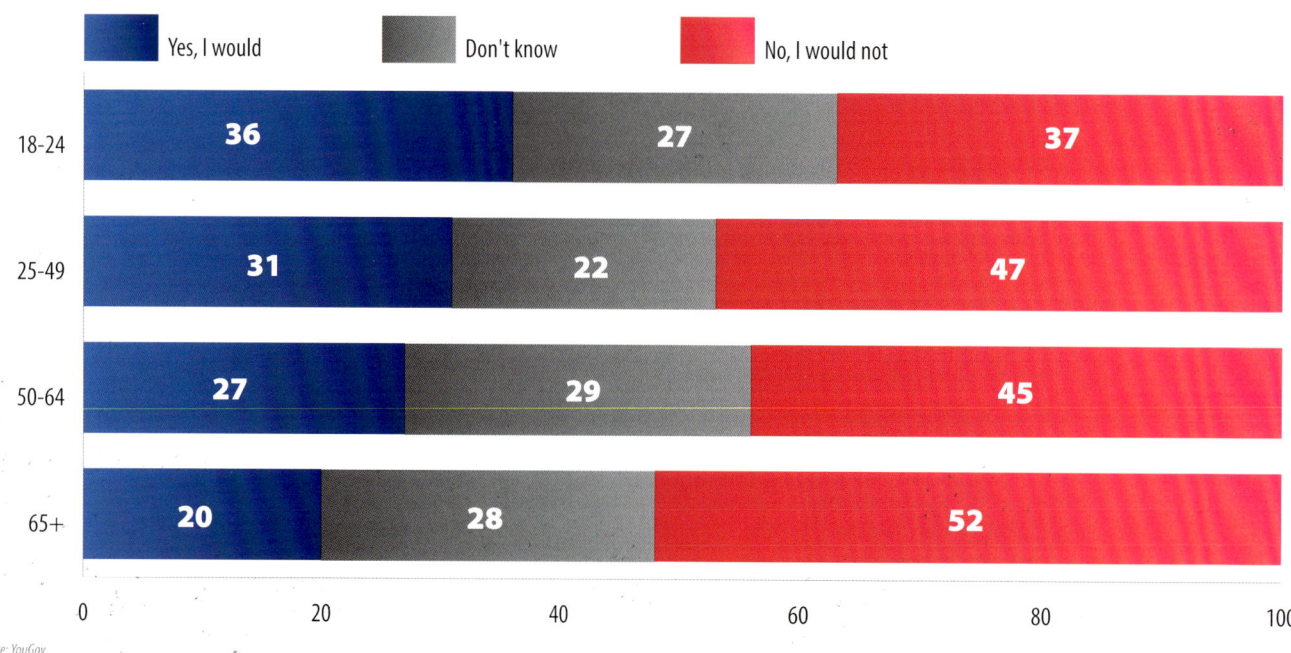

Younger Britons are the most tempted to try CBD products
Would you consider using CBD products? (% of 1428 UK adults who have not tried CBD products before)

Age	Yes, I would	Don't know	No, I would not
18-24	36	27	37
25-49	31	22	47
50-64	27	29	45
65+	20	28	52

Source: YouGov

issues: Discussing Cannabis   36   Chapter 3: Cannabis as Medicine?

Cannabidoil-containing oils are the most popular CBD products with Britons

Which CBD-containing products have you used? (% of UK adults who use CBD products)

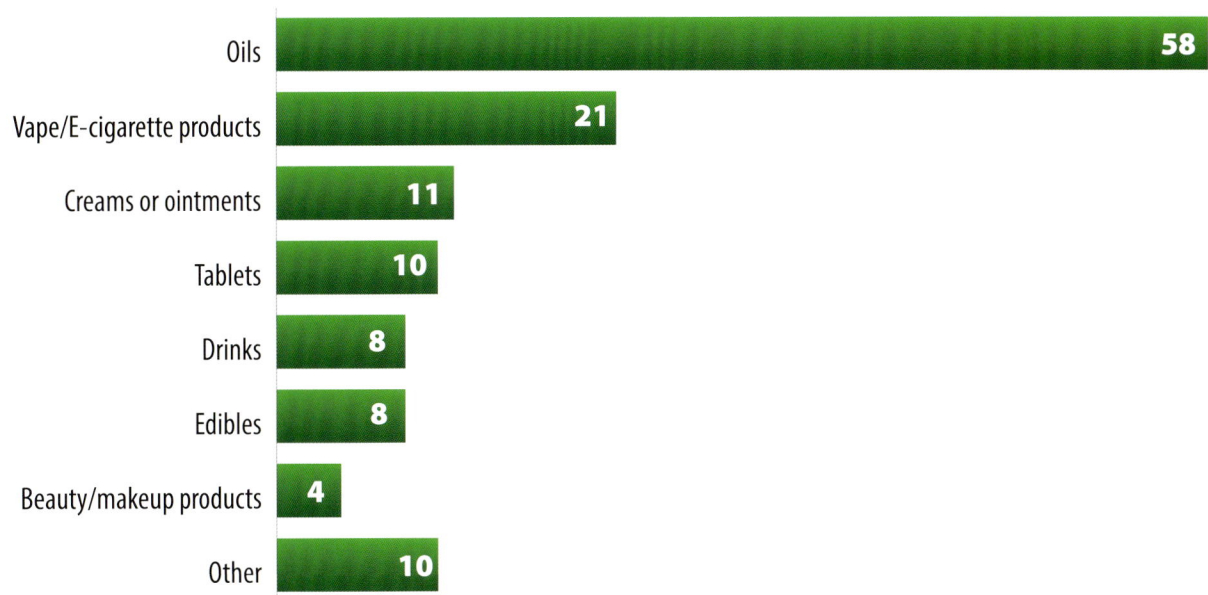

Source: YouGov

Despite their growing popularity amongst big brands, only 4% of those who use CBD products say they use makeup and beauty products which contain the extract.

Over half (61%) of CBD customers say they use the products for medicinal purposes, with pain relief the primary use (71%). Another 38% also say they use the products to treat anxiety and depression.

18 October 2019

The above information is reprinted with kind permission from YouGov.
© 2022 YouGov PLC

www.yougov.co.uk

issues: Discussing Cannabis — Chapter 3: Cannabis as Medicine?

Cannabis has great medical potential. But don't fall for the CBD scam

The UK market for cannabidiol, a compound found in cannabis, will soon be worth £1 billion. But consumers are being conned.

By Mike Power

Roll up, roll up, ladies and gentleman, and gather around. Do you, your loved one – or family pet – suffer from any of the following conditions? Cancer, epilepsy, diabetes, arthritis, anxiety, menstrual cramps, insomnia, dry skin, psychosis, Alzheimer's, dementia, anger, depression, ADHD, Crohn's and IBS, PTSD, opiate addiction, Parkinson's, pain of any kind, migraine, or canine uptightness? Then it's your lucky day.

All can be treated, claim the snake oil salesmen of the modern wild west, with the miracle cure-all: CBD, or cannabidiol. It's one of the 119 cannabinoids contained in cannabis sativa, indica and ruderalis, and all hybrids thereof; aka weed. CBD is legal and doesn't get you high – still-illegal cannabinoid THC does that job very efficiently – but it's fair to say business is blazing.

What a giddy array of products there are: from CBD water (sold in clear bottles that mean the sensitive compound swiftly degrades), to cooking or massage oils, pills, chewing gum, transdermal patches, pessaries, gin, beer and lube. The crown for silliest CBD product of the year, however, belongs indisputably to the CBD-infused pillowcases sold by one hopeful firm of US fabric-makers. Yoga classes offering CBD-assisted asanas and guided meditation have sprung up, with devotees claiming greater flexibility and elevated mood.

Sellers in the UK are careful not to claim any specific medical benefits for the products because of a lack of clinical evidence, so they are instead marketed as food supplements. In this, they are supported by breathless, uncritical media reports on CBD use for airily unspecified 'wellbeing' purposes.

There is now no denying the medicinal value of CBD and THC – not even by the British government, which for years maintained that lie even as it rubber-stamped the cultivation and export of the world's largest medicinal cannabis crop.

But the landmark decision in November 2018 to allow UK doctors to prescribe cannabis under extremely limited circumstances, inspired by the cases of Billy Caldwell and Alfie Dingley, whose epilepsy is improved immeasurably by medicinal cannabis products containing both THC and CBD, has left many in a limbo: knowing or believing that cannabis offers a cure, yet remaining unable to access it.

And so as media reports of miraculous cures for desperate people proliferate, the CBD industry is growing fast. Market research commissioned by the thinktank Centre for Medicinal Cannabis (CMC) estimates that the CBD market in the UK could be worth almost £1 billion a year by 2025, equivalent in size to the current entire UK herbal supplement market.

And in many cases, the industry is taking consumers for a ride. Lab tests for the CMC report analysed high-street offerings and found that more than half of the most popular CBD oils sold do not contain the level of CBD promised on the label. And a look at the label of those products shows that many are sold at such low concentrations that even the guesstimated doses, measured in drops, cannot deliver more than a scant few milligrams of the active ingredient – whereas medical trials use many times more.

Still, mislabelled or low-dose products pale into insignificance when compared to a US case reported in the journal Clinical Toxicology in April. A family unwittingly dosed their child with what was claimed to be CBD oil, but instead contained the synthetic cannabinoid receptor agonist AB-Fubinaca. This chemical is better known as an ingredient in the shortcut to oblivion otherwise known as spice.

Britain is poorly prepared for the wide-ranging changes to cannabis law that are flowering worldwide. British hemp farmers face serious commercial disadvantage as CBD may be legally extracted only from the stem and leaves of hemp crops, not from the flower, where the cannabinoids are produced in greatest profusion. Most CBD is therefore imported: a wasted opportunity to create and control – and tax – a new industry.

What is clear is that legal reform on cannabis, while welcome, is not moving anywhere near quickly enough to benefit millions of patients.

Scientists and politicians are, thankfully, catching up with hundreds of years of folk wisdom: it's not news to anyone who regularly smokes a spliff that cannabis is relaxing, or that it can help you sleep far more soundly than a glass of red wine, or improve your mood. The interplay between THC, CBD, and the hundreds of other active compounds in the cannabis plant could one day be isolated, identified, tested and proven to offer symptomatic help or even a cure for dozens of life-threatening conditions. But decades of pointless prohibition based on specious moral arguments have prevented proper medical research that could have benefited millions.

The CBD market urgently needs proper regulation and more broadly, both the THC and CBD sectors demand the creation of a new medical model that accommodates the complexity of a plant that has been used as a medicine by humans for thousands of years.

Mike Power is a freelance journalist specialising in drugs, science and technology

1 July 2019

The above information is reprinted with kind permission from *The Guardian*.
© 2022 Guardian News and Media Limited

www.theguardian.com

Where can I find help?

Below are some telephone numbers, email addresses and websites of agencies or charities that can offer support or advice if you, or someone you know needs it.

Addaction
addaction.org.uk

Adfam
adfam.org.uk

Amy Winehouse Foundation
0300 30 30 177
amywinehousefoundation.org

Change Grow Live (CGL)
changegrowlive.org

Childline
0800 1111
childline.org.uk

DrugScope
drugscope.org.uk

Dan 24/7 (support in English and Welsh for those in Wales)
0808 80. 2234
Text DAN to 81066
dan247.org.uk

DrugFAM
0300 888 3853 (9am-9pm daily)
drugfam.co.uk

FRANK
Gives confidential advice to anyone concerned about using cannabis or other drugs.
0300 123 6600 (open 24 hours a day)
talktofrank.com

The Mix
0808 808 4994
www.themix.org.uk

Marijuana Anonymous
0300 124 0373
helpline@marijuana-anonymous.org.uk
marijuana-anonymous.org.uk

Narcotics Anonymous
0300 999 1212 (10am – 12 midnight)
ukna.org

Release
ask@release.org.uk
release.org.uk

Samaritans
Call 116 123
jo@samaritans.org
samaritans.org

SFAD - Scottish Families Affected by Alcohol and Drugs
08080 10 10 11
sfad.org.uk

Taking Action on Addiction
actiononaddiction.org.uk

Turning Point
turning-point.co.uk

You can also speak to a trusted adult such as a teacher, or visit your GP who will be able to offer advice, or point you in the right direction to get the help that you need.

Key Facts

- The hallucinogenic effects of cannabis are mainly due to a compound in cannabis called THC (tetrahydrocannabinol) (page 2)

- Cannabis (also known as marijuana, weed, pot, dope or grass) is the most widely used illegal drug in the UK. (page 4)

- Cannabis smoke contains many of the same harmful chemicals found in cigarette smoke. (page 5)

- In 2018, medical marijuana was allowed in Wales, England, and Scotland. (page 8)

- The new study revealed that 31% of young people had tried cannabis and 10% had tried harder drugs by age 17. (page 9)

- Males reported higher rates of cannabis use than females (34% vs 28%). (page 9)

- White teenagers were much more likely to have experimented with substances than their ethnic minority peers. (page 9)

- More than a third (36.7 per cent) of young people aged 16 to 24 admitted to taking illegal drugs including cannabis, cocaine or amphetamines in the past year. (page 11)

- Since the year ending December 1995, cannabis has consistently been the most-used drug in England and Wales. (page 12)

- Cannabis was the most common drug used by young adults. (page 12)

- New research shows that over the past 50 years street cannabis across the world has become substantially stronger carrying an increased risk of harm. (page 13)

- In herbal cannabis, they found that THC concentrations increased by 14% from 1970 to 2017. (page 13)

- Cannabis is the most widely used illicit drug in the world but has recently been legalised in Canada, Uruguay and several states in the USA. (page 13)

- Similar to tobacco, marijuana smoke comprises a variety of toxic chemicals, which are an irritant to your throat and lung. (page 15)

- Cannabis stimulates the appetite, leading to the phenomenon known as 'the munchies'. (page 15)

- Heavy, prolonged use of cannabis can cause paranoia and has been associated with mental health disorders, such as depression and anxiety. (page 15)

- Cannabis users were three times more likely to develop common mental health problems such as depression and anxiety. (page 22)

- Cannabis users were almost 7 times more likely to develop severe mental illnesses such as psychosis or schizophrenia. (page 22)

- Cannabis users are up to five times more likely to have suicidal thoughts than non-smokers, a new study shows. (page 23)

- Female cannabis users were more prone to problematic thoughts. (page 23)

- Recent cannabis use has been shown to affect extremes of nightly sleep duration, being either less than six hours or more than nine hours, with more intense patterns among heavier users. (page 24)

- Cannabis use in North America is increasing, with around 45 million adults in the U.S using it in 2019, which is double the figure reported in the early 2000s. (page 24)

- Cannabis containing tetrahydrocannabinol (THC) affects motor co-ordination and reaction time, can cause hallucination and increases the risk of getting into a collision. (page 27)

- An estimated 200 million people use cannabis across the world. (page 28)

- There's no difference in the risk of developing schizophrenia between both high and low frequency cannabis users. (page 28)

- Both high and low frequency cannabis users were six times more likely to develop schizophrenia compared to those who had never used cannabis. (page 28)

- Adolescence and early adulthood are the most common periods during which people develop schizophrenia. (page 28)

- The $13 billion US cannabis production industry is creating a huge carbon footprint and damaging the environment. (page 29)

- In 2018, laws were changed allowing medical cannabis to be legally prescribed in the UK for the first time. (page 31)

- An estimated 1.4 million people in the UK are using cannabis for medical purposes. (page 31)

- CBD is a non-psychoactive chemical compound found in the marijuana plant. (page 33)

- Side effects of medicinal cannabis can include a decreased appetite, dizziness, fatigue, diarrhoea and nausea. (page 33)

- By 2024, the UK's medicinal cannabis market is predicted to be worth nearly £1.1 billion, while the recreational market is estimated to be around £1.44 billion. (page 35)

- A quarter (28%) say they would consider using products containing CBD. (page 36)

Glossary

Addiction
A dependence on a substance which makes it very difficult to stop taking it. Addiction can be either physical, meaning the user's body has become dependent on the substance and will suffer negative symptoms if the substance is withdrawn, or psychological, meaning a user has no physical need to take a substance, but will experience strong cravings if it is withdrawn.

Cannabidiol (CBD)
Cannabidiol is the second most prevalent active ingredient in cannabis. CBD comes in many forms, including oils, extracts, capsules, patches, vapes, and topical preparations for use on skin. For CBD products to be legal in the UK they must not contain more than 0.2%. CBD can allegedly help with pain, anxiety and cognition, however there is insufficient evidence to support this.

Cannabis
Cannabis is the most widely used illegal drug in Britain. Made from parts of the cannabis plant, it's a naturally occurring drug. It is a mild sedative (often causing a chilled-out feeling or actual sleepiness) and it`s also a mild hallucinogen (meaning users may experience a state where they see objects and reality in a distorted way and may even hallucinate). The main active compound in cannabis is tetrahydrocannabinol (THC). Slang names include dope, ganja, grass, hash, marijuana, weed and pot.

Herbal cannabis (grass or weed)
This is made from the dried leaves and flowering parts of the female plant and looks like tightly packed dried herbs.

Medicinal cannabis
There is evidence that cannabis use alleviates the painful symptoms of some diseases, such as Multiple Sclerosis and Arthritis. This is a controversial subject, as many believe those with debilitating illness should not be prosecuted if they are using cannabis for pain relief. However, others say that the law must apply to everyone or its impact is weakened.

Misuse of Drugs Act 1971
Legislation prohibiting the use of dangerous recreational substances, making it an offence to possess banned drugs for personal use or with the intent to supply. It also divides drugs into three classes according to the degree of harm they pose to the individual and to society – A, B or C – each with different associated penalties.

Multiple Sclerosis (MS)
A condition of the central nervous system in which the immune system attacks itself.

Psychoactive Drug
A drug that affects the brain function; often resulting in changes of mood, behaviour or perception-levels.

Psychosis
A mental state in which the perception of reality is distorted.

Reclassification
When an illegal substance is moved from one drugs class into another, after its harmfulness has been reassessed or new research has uncovered previously-unknown negative effects. For example, cannabis has been reclassified twice in the past decade, being moved from Class B to Class C in 2004 and back to Class B again in 2009.

Recreational Drug
A drug that is taken occasionally and is often claimed to be non-addictive.

Resin (hash)
`Hash` is a blackish-brown lump made from the resin of the cannabis plant. In the past, this was the commonest form of cannabis in the UK, but this is no longer the case. Herbal cannabis (and especially powerful skunk strains) is now the most common form of cannabis used in the UK.

Risky Behaviour
Behaviour that has the potential to get out of control or become dangerous.

Schizophrenia
Disorder characterised by hallucinations, paranoid delusions and abnormal thought patterns.

Skunk
This is a high-strength herbal cannabis. There is evidence that skunk has been increasing in THC content over the past three decades, resulting in stronger, more harmful cannabis. While previously resin was more common, skunk now dominates the UK cannabis market. Although the term `skunk` was originally applied to specific strains of strong-smelling herbal cannabis, the term is now often applied to any type of very potent herbal cannabis.

THC
THC is an abbreviation of delta-9-tetrahydrocannabinol. This is the main psychoactive ingredient in cannabis and leads to the feeling of being `stoned`. The higher the concentration of this chemical, the more potent the strain of cannabis. It is because of this ingredient that cannabis is one of the most easily detectable drugs when carrying out drugs tests, as THC can take weeks to clear from the body.

Activities

Brainstorming

- Brainstorm what you know about cannabis.
    - What is cannabis?
        - What is THC?
        - What is CBD?
- What effects can cannabis have on people's health?
- What risks can cannabis use have?
- What conditions/illnesses can medicinal cannabis help?

Research

- Do some research into the usage of cannabis in the UK compared with other countries in the world. Create an infographic or map showing your findings.
- Do some research into the medical uses of cannabis and the conditions it is used to treat. Write a one-page article about your findings.
- In pairs, research the effects that cannabis use has on mental health. Show your findings in a presentation.
- In small groups, research medicinal cannabis and the conditions that it can help. Present your findings on a poster.
- Research the countries that allow recreational or medicinal use of cannabis, and those where it is illegal. Present your findings in a map.
- Research the risks that cannabis has to the user. This could be mentally or physically.
- Research people's views on CBD products. Try to ask a broad range of people; are there any differences in views between the ages or genders?

Design

- Choose one article from this book and design an infographic to display the key theme of the article.
- Choose one of the articles and create an illustration.
- Design a leaflet to highlight the risks to your health if you use cannabis.
- Design a poster to show the risks of 'drug driving'.
- Design a 'signposting' poster for people who need to seek help with their cannabis use. Include at least three charities or organisations that can help.
- Design a poster to show the effects that cannabis can have on the body or brain.
- Design an app to help people who are trying to stop using cannabis. What can you include to prevent them from using the drug? Consider the cost of the app, would it be free to use?

Oral

- As a class, discuss the pros and cons of legalising cannabis.
- In small groups, discuss why people who are ill may want to use cannabis.
- In pairs, talk about CBD and where and which products you have seen it in. Make a list of the things and which type of shop they are found in.
- As a class, discuss whether you think using cannabis will lead to people using 'harder' drugs.
- Split the class into two; half will be for the use of medicinal cannabis and half will be against.
- In small groups, discuss whether or not cannabis can have an effect on your academic performance.

Reading/Writing

- Choose one article from this book and write a one paragraph summary. Pick out three key points.
- Write a letter to an agony aunt/uncle. Imagine that you are concerned about a friend's use of cannabis. Then, write a reply with some advice that you could offer to the friend.
- Write an article for your school newspaper about the medical use of cannabis. You should list the conditions it might be used to treat and should give your views as to whether you feel it would be appropriate for the NHS to fund its use in this way.
- Write a persuasive letter to either argue against or for the legalisation of cannabis. Include reasons such as effects on health, effects on the environment, money or anything else that can support your idea.
- Choose an article in this book, write an article in response to either support or argue against their ideas.

Index

A
academic performance 18–19
addiction 3, 4, 13, 17, 21, 41
alcohol 9–10
amphetamines 11, 22
antisocial behaviours 10

B
binge drinking 9–10
blood, effects of cannabis 15
bongs 1
brain, effects of cannabis 2, 14–15, 16

C
cannabis
    and academic performance 18–19
    addiction 3, 4, 13, 17, 21, 41
    cut-with substances 3
    decriminalising 6–7
    and driving 3, 26
    duration of effects 2, 15
    edibles 1–2, 27
    effects of 2, 4, 14–28
    giving up 4
    hangover from 17
    inhalation methods 1–2, 27
    and the law 3, 6–8, 11, 13, 18
    medical use 5, 6–8, 15, 30–38
    and mental health 3, 4–5, 15, 21–25, 28
    misuse 11–12, 23
    mixing with other drugs 3
    and pregnancy 5, 15
    risks 2–3, 4–5
    and sleep 24
    smoking 1, 2–3
    strength of 13
    and suicidal thoughts 23
    types of 1
    use by men and boys 9, 23
    use by teenagers and young people 9–12, 18
    use by women and girls 9, 23
    vaping 2
cannabis oil 1
cannabis use disorder 23
CBD (cannabidiol) 2, 5, 13, 30–33, 36–38, 41
    see also medical use
CBD products 36–38
cigarettes 9, 15
Class B drugs 3, 6–8
cocaine 11, 12, 22
Crime Survey for England and Wales 11

D
dab 1
decriminalising cannabis 6–7
derealisation disorder 25
dissociative disorders 25
driving, and cannabis 3, 26

E
ecstasy 12
edibles 1–2, 27
epilepsy 31–33

G
Generation Z, Millennium Cohort Study (MCS) 9–10

H
hallucinations 2, 4, 15
hangovers 17
hash (hashish) 1, 13, 41
health, effects of cannabis 15
herbal cannabis 13, 41
heroin 22

L
legislation
    cannabis worldwide 6, 8, 13, 18, 26
    Class B drugs 3, 6–8
lethargy 2
lungs, effects of cannabis 15

M
marijuana *see* cannabis
medicinal cannabis 5, 6–8, 15, 30–38, 41
mental health 3, 4–5, 15, 21–25, 28
Millennium Cohort Study (MCS) 9–10
Misuse of Drugs Act 1971 41
multiple sclerosis (MS) 5, 15, 34, 41

O
Office for National Statistics (ONS), *Crime Survey for England and Wales* 11

P
paranoia 2
pregnancy 5, 15
psychoactive drug 41
psychosis 21, 22, 30, 41
psychotic illnesses 4–5, 13, 21–22, 31

R
reclassification 41
resin *see* hash (hashish)
risks, of using cannabis 2–3, 4–5

S
schizophrenia 4–5, 21–22, 28, 31, 41
shatter 1
skunk 1, 41
sleep 24
smoking cannabis 1, 2–3
spliffs (joints) 1
suicidal thoughts 23
suicide 23
sustainability, and cannabis production 29

T
THC (tetrahydrocannabinol) 2, 5, 13, 14–15, 17, 19, 20, 27, 30, 33, 41
tobacco 9, 15

V
vaping cannabis 2

W
weed 1
    see also cannabis

Acknowledgements

The publisher is grateful for permission to reproduce the material in this book. While every care has been taken to trace and acknowledge copyright, the publisher tenders its apology for any accidental infringement or where copyright has proved untraceable. The publisher would be pleased to come to a suitable arrangement in any such case with the rightful owner.

The material reproduced in **issues** books is provided as an educational resource only. The views, opinions and information contained within reprinted material in **issues** books do not necessarily represent those of Independence Educational Publishers and its employees.

Images

Cover image courtesy of iStock. All other images courtesy Freepik, Pixabay & Unsplash.

Illustrations

Simon Kneebone: pages 4, 14 & 20. Angelo Madrid: pages 9, 22 & 37.

Additional acknowledgements

Page 9: Fitzsimons, E. and Villadsen, A. (2021) *Substance use and antisocial behaviour in adolescence: Evidence from the UK Millennium Cohort Study at age 17*. London: Centre for Longitudinal Studies

With thanks to the Independence team: Shelley Baldry, Tracy Biram and Jackie Staines.

Danielle Lobban

Cambridge, January 2022